CARDS
ON THE TABLE
WOKING'S CONFERENCE YEARS

CARDS
ON THE TABLE
WOKING'S CONFERENCE YEARS

Clive Youlton & Paul Beard

Foreword by Martin Tyler

TEMPUS

Frontispiece: Goalscorers Colin Fielder and Scott Steele show off the FA Trophy after the 1995 triumph.

First published 2003

Tempus Publishing Ltd
The Mill, Brimscombe Port
Stroud, Gloucestershire GL5 2QG
www.tempus-publishing.com

British Library Cataloguing in Publication Data.
A catalogue record for this book is available from the British Library.

ISBN 0 7524 2580 3

Typesetting and origination by Tempus Publishing.
Printed in Great Britain by Midway Colour Print, Wiltshire

Contents

Acknowledgements

We would like to thank the following for their assistance in the completion of this book. Woking Football Club and the club's photographer, Tony Charters for the use of photographs. Gary Letts, freelance photographer, also for the use of photographs. The *Woking News and Mail* for quotes used from previous editions of the newspaper. Martin Tyler, who was recently voted Premiership commentator of the decade by TV viewers, for kindly agreeing to write the foreword, thus giving the book some real credibility. Chris Ingram, chairman of the club, for his support for the book and agreeing for it to be made official, as well as for writing a contribution. To James Howarth, Tempus Publishing and in particular Vivien Lambe for making the book possible. To our other halves, Nicola Youlton and Jessica Sharpe, for putting up with countless long nights in front of the television while we were busy on our computers. And last but by no means least, to Justine Stevenson, former editor of the *Woking News and Mail*, for her tireless work in proof reading every word in her own time and her patience in doing so.

A Word from the Chairman

I am delighted that Clive Youlton and Paul Beard have combined together to produce this recent history of Woking Football Club. The Conference Years have probably been the most exciting period in the history of The Cards. We have had great success in the FA Trophy, enjoyed sensational upsets in the FA Cup and in the league, had to deal with the stress of near promotion and relegation. All in a ten year period! Clive and Paul give you the inside story on many of the incidents for the first time but always in the spirit of true fans of the club.

Enjoy!

Chris Ingram
Chairman
Woking Football Club

Foreword

You could almost write an entire book about the events at Kingfield on Saturday April 26 2003, so *Cards on the Table – Woking FC The Conference Years* has a rich vein of material and Clive Youlton and Paul Beard have expertly brought it to the surface. Geoff Chapple made the story possible by lifting the club from its Isthmian League roots to the highest level it has ever attained and came so close to fulfilling his dreams of managing The Cards in the Football League, though those three Wembley wins in four seasons did offer substantial consolation. Letting go of Geoff and the on the field class of Clive Walker at the same time in 1997 was very bad business. Even a man as steeped in football as John McGovern, a European Cup-winning captain no less, found their act hard to follow. Brian McDermott, who had been taught the game at Highbury, worked tirelessly but could not turn the tide. Therefore the more recent tales have been of survival rather than the pursuit of promotion. It has been very nerve-wracking on television gantries up and down the Premiership waiting for someone to let me know the results. Colin Lippiatt's five wins in a row at the latter stages of the 99-00 season made the impossible possible. Glenn Cockerill has now come into the same category as the Houdini manager of 2003. I am a great believer that you have to experience the tough times to really appreciate the more prosperous periods. Over the 11 years the standard of Conference football has risen considerably. Confronting teams that have been training full-time has been very difficult, and now thanks to Chris Ingram's investment it is a case of if we can't beat them let's join them. A new era is about to begin at Woking Football Club. The inside story of its predecessor is splendidly packaged in the ensuing pages.

Martin Tyler
President of Woking FC Supporters Club
June 2003

Introduction

The reason Paul Beard and I came to write this book is a simple one. It would be satisfying to admit that the idea came from a deep desire within to chronicle what is a fascinating period in Woking Football Club's history. Or even to say that the inevitable disappointment of being ultimately ushered out of at least one publisher's office was outweighed by the hope that one such company would be persuaded of the book's merits. The truth is far less romantic. It was because I was asked. It is not every day that a publisher rings you up out of the blue and says, 'Do you want to write a book about Woking Football Club?' but that is exactly what happened. The man on the end of the phone was James Howarth of Tempus Publishing in Stroud but, convinced it was a wind up allied to the fact that such a task would involve a lot of time and effort, my reaction was muted to say the least. It transpired that James' boss at the time, Stephen Lambe, is the cousin of Vivien Lambe, a colleague of mine who just happened to throw my name into the hat when the subject of finding an author for a Woking book was mentioned. It really is a small world.

Having decided to write about the Conference years I knew I couldn't do it without the help of someone involved at Kingfield, not least because 50,000 words is quite an undertaking while I also didn't have the detailed knowledge of those first five seasons. Enter Paul, who was not only happy to get involved but also discreet enough to ensure the project remained a well-kept secret for nigh on a year. Paul wrote the opening five chapters including Geoff Chapple's last in 1996/97, while I wrote the final six, from John McGovern's first year in 1997/98 right through until the end of 2002/03, last season. The result is one that I hope does justice to what is a fascinating story – one that ended with those dramatic events on April 26 this year. But before we embark on the Conference years it is important to remember just how Woking arrived in non-League's top division and just what a household name the club had become thanks to the exploits of Tim Buzaglo and company. The Cards' reputation had been built on those wonderful FA Cup exploits in 1990/91 and the following season saw league attendance's steadily increase from around 1,400 to more than 2,000. Indeed Enfield and Kingstonian attracted more than 3,000 to Kingfield as the Diadora League Championship was won at a canter. It didn't seem to matter that Geoff Chapple's men failed to record a league win in their final six matches of that 1991/1992 season, the championship having been sewn up with four weeks and seven matches to spare. At one stage The Cards led their nearest rivals by 26 points and they eventually finished an incredible 18 points ahead of Enfield, who had been crushed 5-0 at Kingfield in November. Names such as Adie Cowler, Stewart Mitchell, Andy Parr, Andy Russell, George Friel, Nick Collier, Francis Vines and Bradley Pratt were synonymous with the achievements and the great strides the club had made. But none of them were destined to further their careers with

Jubilant players looking out for friends and relatives after the dramatic 1-1 draw at Coventry City in 1997.

Woking's Geoff Chapple and Kidderminster's Graham Allner lead out their teams for the 1995 FA Trophy final at Wembley.

Woking. Laurence Batty, Trevor Baron, Dereck Brown and Mark Biggins, all legends in their day, were the only four players in the first Conference starting line-up from the team that played in the final match of the previous season. It really was a case of all change as a new chapter in the club's history dawned, but The Cards' roots had been firmly established. In essence a bunch of local part-timers had made an indelible mark at Kingfield and to a wider football audience, attracting the next generation of Woking followers in the process. The game was about to become big business with the advent of the Premiership coinciding with The Cards' rise to prominence in the non-League game. Where would the next breed of players take the club? How would Woking fare in the Conference and what would the age of professionalism bring? The answers are hopefully encapsulated in the following chapters, in what has turned out to be a real roller-coaster ride for the hardcore of supporters who have stuck with their club through thick and thin. We enjoyed writing this book and are delighted Woking Football Club backed us in making it official. Hopefully you will enjoy it too and end up thinking 'thanks for the memories' – albeit that some of them are best forgotten.

Clive Youlton
June 2003

1

In the Beginning
1992/93

In the summer of 1992, Woking strode into the Conference full of confidence after a season which had proved something of a cakewalk – the Isthmian League title being won on a memorable afternoon in Windsor weeks before the end of the previous campaign. It was to prove the start of a long and unbroken association at the helm of the non-League game, with both highs and lows in equal measure during an 11-year period (to date). But for most of the players who had achieved such unprecedented success it was the end of the road as Cards boss Geoff Chapple decided wholesale change was not only necessary but vital if the club was going to progress further.

On the advice of his old friend John Still, manager of Dagenham & Redbridge, Chapple decided to dismantle the side that had performed so well for him in breezing to promotion. With the help of his assistant, Colin Lippiatt, the boss drafted in the experienced players it was said were needed to survive at Conference level. Chapple signed some well-known names – but many questioned whether they were needed. Would they have the same passion and hunger as those local lads who had brushed aside virtually every non-League challenge the previous season? On paper the new recruits would bring what was required but teams do not win things on paper and the acid test would come against seasoned Conference clubs, with plenty of wise old heads and more than a few giants scattered among them.

Even though big names had been recruited at Kingfield, there was some disquiet from fans over the way the likes of Adie Cowler, an inspirational captain, had been excluded from Chapple's plans. Surely the majority of the side that had served the club so well deserved to sample the fruits of what their labours had achieved. At the very least shouldn't they be able to prove themselves capable of doing the job? But Chapple had worked wonders before, now it was time for the 'terrace managers' to show faith in his judgement. So, there would no longer be the likes of Andy Russell, Stewart Mitchell and Bradley Pratt. In came the new breed.

Trevor Senior was brought in, a man who had set scoring records more or less where-ver he had been, enjoying a particularly good time at Reading. Dave Puckett had played alongside seven England international captains during his time with Southampton while Robbie Carroll had a proven pedigree, as did Andy Clement. The latter, who had enjoyed a brief spell with Woking previously, had been involved in the FA Charity Shield for Wimbledon against Liverpool. Another newcomer, Kevan Brown, had played for a number of clubs and was with Aldershot when they folded, but what an inspirational signing he later proved to be. Richard Nugent had won the Conference title with Barnet and Mark Fleming came to the club from QPR via Farnborough Town.

A hugely significant signing was that of the wispy Scott Steele. The story goes that Chapple saw a video of the youngster from north of the border while he was playing for Airdrie and was so impressed by what he saw that – a bit like Victor Kiam and the electronic shaver – he 'bought the product'. Steele, like Brown, went on to become a Woking legend despite looking far too small and lightweight to compete against some of the giants that most teams packed their defences with. Such was Chapple's desire to keep Steele at the club that he allowed the hugely popular Scot to live in his family home at Farnham, treating him almost like a son.

The summer was busy for those not concerned with improving the playing staff. Serious doubts were cast as to whether or not the Conference ground requirements would be met. Many anxious eyes watched the progress on the Chris Lane Terrace and the Westfield Avenue turnstiles and other areas of the ground that needed improvement. With limited time to do the work, ground and safety officer Paul Elmer appeared to toil night and day to ensure that everything that needed to be done was actually accomplished. His efforts on behalf of the club that summer should never be underestimated.

Chapple had shown a voracious appetite when it came to signing players and a pre-season trip to Aldershot had him again reaching for the transfer forms. Like Chapple, supporters watching the game were impressed with a young defender by the name of Tony Joyce. Little did they know that Chapple would deliver on his promise to "get him to Woking". By the time the opening match of the season arrived, a certain Mr Joyce was a Card. As well as the new faces that were brought in to do the business on the pitch, the club had a new commercial manager. Chris Richardson, a former service-man who had played football for the Army and whom Chapple described as being in a different class to the other candidates for the post, was appointed.

Robbie Carroll tussles for possession against Brentford in a pre-season friendly.

George Friel – Goal-getter.

His influence was seen in the first match of the season. Half-time entertainment came in the shape of Rob Walters, a cousin of then Liverpool winger Mark Walters, described in the programme as a world record holder for his football juggling tricks and the like. All good stuff – but was it really what the fans wanted to see? As it happened it was his only appearance at the ground. Thankfully Richardson didn't feel it necessary to go further and recruit the likes of the Dagenham Girl Pipers. The gimmick of extra-curricula activities didn't catch on and half-time soon returned to being dedicated to first-half musing and the supping of drinks.

Richardson found sponsorship for the number of goals scored but, as has often been the way, that well-meaning initiative failed to catch the imagination of the supporters. However, he did breathe much-needed life into the club shop, introducing a number of new lines that helped promote the club. In particular, the cufflinks that he arranged were on sale for a number of years and certainly stayed around a lot longer than Richardson himself (or indeed a number of the many players that Chapple signed).

"We must be under no illusions as to the daunting task that awaits us in the Conference", was Geoff Chapple's opening gambit in the matchday programme for the visit of Stafford Rangers on Saturday 22 August 1992. As it transpired they were fairly prophetic words but surely even Chapple didn't seriously believe his newly assembled side would learn such a harsh lesson in the first 90 minutes of the season. A team that struggled to avoid relegation from the Conference in the previous campaign brushed his charges aside and the 3-0 scoreline in Stafford's favour could so easily have read 8-0 or worse – the visitors missing a penalty and striking the woodwork on at least four occasions. Almost as shocking as the result were the shirts that the Woking players donned: quite who came up with the idea of pink with white blotches is anybody's guess but to say they looked out of place is surely an understatement.

The mercurial Mark Biggins in action in the Championship Shield clash against Grays Athletic.

Woking found their Conference feet in their first midweek game of the campaign, although the match very nearly didn't take place. Kettering Town were in financial difficulties and there was the distinct possibility that the match at Rockingham Road would be called off. Fleming scored the only goal of the game, from the penalty spot, to get the first points on the board. However, joy returned to deep gloom on the second Saturday of the season when Stalybridge Celtic, also in their first season of Conference football, won 3-0 amongst the rolling hills on the very edge of Greater Manchester. By this time there had already been player changes, with John Finch vanishing after the first game and George Friel – whose goals were plentiful and meaningful in 1991/92 – having gone to Slough Town in exchange for Colin Fielder.

The topsy-turvy pattern for the season was established as once again fans had something to celebrate on Bank Holiday Monday. The trophy cabinet was boosted when Grays Athletic were comprehensively beaten 5-1 in the Isthmian Charity Shield. FA Cup hero Tim Buzaglo picked up a brace in that match and repeated the trick a few days later when his pace proved altogether too much for Runcorn, who were sunk 4-0 in The Cards' first Conference win at Kingfield.

In his notes for the Runcorn game Chapple, clearly taken aback by the unconvincing start to the season, said: "I would ask for a little patience in these early days, as we strive to adjust to the superior standards required just to even survive in the Conference". The Bob Lord Trophy has had a whole series of names over the years and in 1992/93 it was known as The Drinkwise Cup. The first round was a two-legged affair and Woking's first opponents were Welling United. They won 2-1 at Kingfield and although Senior scored his first goal for the club in the return leg two weeks later, the 2-2 draw saw Woking bow out 4-3 on aggregate.

The first ever visit to Telford United a few days later looked like being a turning point, with goals from Trevor Baron, Mark Biggins and Puckett putting Woking in the driving seat. However, scoring three was one thing – letting three in at the other end was just as likely and that is exactly what happened. Half-time was unusual, Chapple and loyal lieutenant Lippiatt keeping all the players on the pitch throughout the break. Was it the fact that the dressing rooms were not good enough? Could it be that they all preferred the open air? Or was it the fact that a public dressing down was the identified remedy? Who knows? The fact is that it was the only time the 'tactic' was employed.

Altrincham was the next side to test The Cards' resolve and a reminder of how they kept Woking at bay haunted the club for the rest of the season, with the matchday programme cover photograph showing an 'Alti' defender easily keeping Puckett – quite literally – at arm's length. In that game, as in many others in this inaugural season at the top, the opposition successfully employed smash-and-grab tactics after being second best in terms of skill and possession. With less than two months of the season gone it was clear that Woking needed to toughen up, even though that may have been at the cost of some of the traditional flair that both Chapple and Lippiatt had built their formidable reputations on.

Things looked pretty bleak when the side crashed 5-1 at Dagenham & Redbridge. Worse still was the fact that flamboyant keeper 'Lol' Batty was sent off and Trev 'The Perm' Senior came off the bench to go in goal. But the mood was lifted when Puckett, with the only goal of the game, ensured a home win over Northwich Victoria. And by

Former Saint Dave Puckett on the ball against Altrincham.

the time the team faced Bromsgrove Rovers at Kingfield a week later, two familiar Woking diehards were back in the side. Lloyd and Shane Wye, local legends and veterans of the Isthmian-winning side, were back from New Zealand where they had been playing in the national league. Chapple reportedly picked the players up from the airport, and ensured Lloyd was provided with some boots. Despite their presence another defeat was recorded, again against a side 'enjoying' their first season of Conference football. Having lost to both of the clubs that had been promoted with them, and without a goal against either, Woking's future did not look too rosy at the end of October.

On account of his red card at Dagenham, Batty had been unavailable for the Bromsgrove game and he was still suspended when the side succumbed 4-1 to Yeovil Town. Even at this early stage the prospect of relegation loomed large. After the decisive defeat at Yeovil it was time to turn the attentions to the FA Cup, the competition that had put The Cards in the spotlight a couple of seasons earlier, with heroics against West Bromwich Albion and Everton. Nuneaton Borough were the visitors and with Woking reduced to ten men, 2-1 down and only minutes to play, the signs were not good. However, two late, late goals conjured up an improbable 3-2 win and an away tie against Brighton and Hove Albion. Carroll, Clement and Biggins were the men on target, Biggins having survived Chapple's cull in the summer.

Chapple is not normally one to speak out against officials but was minded to do so on this occasion. Discussing the dismissal of Baron, he said: "Once again we saw yet

Striker Trevor Senior makes his presence felt at Telford United.

another refereeing decision that quite simply staggered me. I thought Trevor went for the ball and actually won it before his opponent fell over his legs. We await the video with interest." Presumably the video was not too interesting as Baron served his suspension and that was the last quote on the subject from the manager.

Next came Gateshead, another side who left Kingfield with all three points after cashing in on the profligacy of the Woking defence and a moment of madness from Batty, who was caught out of goal somewhere near the centre line on the Woking right and lobbed from distance. The omens were not good, although the match did mark a first Conference goal for Senior.

An oasis in a desert of regular defeats came with a 5-1 mauling of Merthyr Tydfil in front of their own fans. Senior grabbed a brace, as did Steve Milton. Quite why Milton didn't get many more opportunities in the team is something of a mystery as, along with Friel, he had scored more than enough to warrant a chance at the higher level.

The game in Wales marked the debut of a young central defender from Wimbledon. Tim Alexander, who had grown up in the Woking area, filled in for the suspended Baron and went on to have a storming season in place of the man who had been such a favourite. Alexander was an inspirational signing and Senior too began to find his inspiration. Once he had found where the nets were on Conference grounds he started to home in on them and in a somewhat surprising 2-1 win away to Boston United, he notched his fourth in three games. It is easy to imagine what he could have done if there had been wide players able to put the ball onto his head time after time.

Massed ranks of Cards' fans at Brighton in the FA Cup.

More encouraging signs came in the second contest against Dagenham & Redbridge as Carroll scored the goal that won a point in the last game before the FA Cup tie at Brighton. The Seagulls had all sorts of financial problems but they also had some big names and were clear favourites to end Woking's interest in the road to Wembley. Among the Brighton ranks was a certain Clive Walker, a name that was to become synonymous with Woking, flowing non-League football and success.

Walker was marked by Clement and the former Wimbledon player kept him very quiet. Shane Wye scored a second-half equaliser to bring the teams back to Kingfield. The importance of the replay was demonstrated by a crowd not far short of 6,000. They watched as Senior scored to put Woking ahead. However, Walker inspired his side to come from behind to win and earn themselves a home tie against Portsmouth in the third round.

Two Conference games had separated the FA Cup matches and four vital points were picked up in the space of five days – with a draw at Welling and a win at Runcorn. 12 December 1992 will go down in history as the day that Woking recorded their first Conference double – just how many Runcorn fans know that fact? More to the point, it may not have registered with too many Woking fans either.

Boston made their first visit to Kingfield and found themselves denied by an outstanding display in goal by newcomer Danny Honey. He had been at Reading and was drafted in to replace the unavailable Batty on the recommendation of Senior. Puckett proved that, just like London buses, one double can become a brace of doubles and the Lincolnshire outfit went home comprehensively beaten. One of the goals was probably the freakiest that Puckett, or anyone else for that matter, ever scored. It came

Trevor Senior snapping at the heels of the Runcorn defenders.

from virtually the halfway line when he charged down a clearance from Boston keeper Paul Bastock and saw the ball loop from in front of the dugouts into the empty net at the end which now houses the impressive Leslie Gosden Stand.

The period just after Christmas saw Wycombe Wanderers, packed full of star players and led by Martin O'Neill, trounce The Cards 3-0, while the win at Slough Town was more memorable for the fact that the referee had still not blown the final whistle by 5 p.m.

Surely Dorking would not prove too much of a problem in the Surrey Senior Cup? Sadly this was not the case. After a 2-2 draw on the mudbath that was Meadowbank, they came to Kingfield and won 2-0, ending all interest in that particular competition. Less than 96 hours later the FA Trophy too was of purely academic interest following an appallingly inept performance away to Sutton United, a side that had been relegated from the Conference. Chapple was not a happy man after the defeat and could not have been more accurate when he said: "There can be no excuses whatsoever. On the day we were completely outplayed and furthermore, if the home side had taken their chances the scoreline would at least have been double." While wishing Sutton good luck in the competition, he went on to say: "We need to have a good look at ourselves, because although we have the quality we will achieve nothing unless we show the commitment, passion and will to win. I'll save the other adjectives for the dressing room."

In his notes for the game at home to Welling United, Chapple, whose side were at the time third in the form table and seventh in the league, had a swipe at the players when he wrote: "Judging by our last two performances we are in a very false position in the Conference because our present form has been one of a side that looks to be in the relegation zone". Surely the day would never dawn when that claim would turn out to be true?

As it turned out Fleming, with a penalty, secured all three points that afternoon and Senior grabbed another in a 1-1 draw at the impressive but sparsely populated International Stadium in Gateshead. Woking's support had become legendary during the early years of Chapple's tenure and he was moved to write for the next home game, against Yeovil Town:

I would sincerely like to say a big thank you to our supporters for your tremendous support at Gateshead last Saturday. The Gateshead officials were taken aback and had never seen anything like it for a football match at the International Stadium before.

One wonders, given that the attendance was a somewhat paltry figure of 626, if the officials there had any experience of a real football crowd. Certainly they could not have been to Kingfield before. Nevertheless, Chapple's comments were typically generous and aimed at a group of fans with whom he enjoyed a fantastic mutually appreciative relationship.

Midway through February, there was some light relief from the competitive football when Kispest-Honved, who included no less than ten Hungarian internationals in their side, came to Kingfield. Somewhat optimistically – or perhaps with his tongue firmly in

Richard Nugent and Trevor Baron getting up and at 'em.

his cheek – Chapple wrote: "It is hoped that in the near future we may be able to organise a return trip to Budapest, certainly we will be discussing the possibilities this evening with the Honved directors". It never happened and perhaps something was lost in the translation, or was it the fact that nobody actually fancied the goulash? Whatever the reason, the trip was never mentioned again, despite the fact that Woking won the match 2-1.

Euphoria returned with an emphatic 4-0 home win against Macclesfield Town. Carroll had not had too many opportunities to show what he could do but scored again and earned a glowing tribute from Chapple: "I've yet to see anyone quicker than him this year and I must admit that he has given us a selection headache because with the injured players fast recovering, he has certainly done enough to stay in the side". He was to make another six appearances, two of which were as a substitute.

However, it was back to the yo-yo cycle the following week as Merthyr Tydfil won 2-0 at Kingfield, although very few people went away from the ground actually talking about the football, the fact that Steele missed a penalty or the final result itself. The talk was of Lloyd Wye, playing his last game before returning to New Zealand, who was sent off for striking David D'Auria. Unfortunately, the incident did not end with Lloyd vanishing down the tunnel. He found himself in trouble with the boys in blue after D'Auria made a complaint of assault against him. The inspirational left-back, just like his brother Shane, had Woking carved right through him and it was impossible not to feel sorry for him despite the fact he was clearly in the wrong. His commitment had done the club proud for a long time and this was a momentary lapse that should not eclipse fans' memories of his loyal service. If only his spirit, never mind his ability, could be bottled and infused into all that are lucky enough to wear a Woking shirt.

In springtime Chapple had more than football results to think about, with his wife Sally giving birth to a daughter, Lucy. In years to come young Lucy was naturally an important factor in Chapple's bid for job security. Defeats against Altrincham and Slough Town, followed by a 0-0 draw away to Stafford Rangers and a stirring 3-2 home win against Kettering Town, were next in Woking's mixed bag of a season. Kettering was a thoroughly entertaining affair, but then Nugent scored an own goal to ensure that Bath City went home with a win under their belts and Mike Deavin, programme editor at the time, was just one who voiced the opinion that relegation was still an option.

That threat was abated by a pulsating 3-2 win at home to Telford United, after being 3-0 ahead at half-time. This followed a draw away to Macclesfield Town, which ended in tragedy for Paul Kelly. On loan from Fulham, Kelly had enjoyed a fine match for Woking but in the early hours of the following morning he was involved in a fatal road accident, in which his best friend died. That put football firmly into perspective.

Kidderminster Harriers paid a visit on Grand National Day. They had been, believe it or not, in danger of being relegated, but there was not much sign of it as they cruised to a somewhat emphatic 5-1 win. That, as all sporting aficionados will know, was not the only farce that day, the Grand National being abandoned when the starter made a blunder. What Woking would have given for a similar decision regarding the result at Kingfield.

Kevan Brown – Captain Marvel.

The prospect of visiting Wycombe Wanderers, who had clinched their promotion spot at a canter, was not one to be relished. However, in front of a packed Adams Park crowd, Chapple's side made amends in some style and outplayed the champions in a highly entertaining 0-0 draw. Sadly the match marked the end of Alexander's loan spell, a period in which he greatly endeared himself to fans, fellow players and officials alike.

The club went into the final home game of the season, a fixture that ended with a revenge win against Stalybridge Celtic, with nine of the players who had featured in the squad for the clash against Stafford way back in August. By the final day of the campaign, Woking travelled to Bromsgrove knowing they had done enough to secure another campaign at the top of the non-League tree. The West Midlands side were enjoying life in the Conference and their 1-0 win, coupled with results elsewhere, meant that they finished as runners-up to Wycombe. Naturally enough their players, fans and officials were cock-a-hoop over what they had achieved, but it was surely not the done thing for the referee to join in the celebrations? It was not that anybody hinted at there being any impropriety – it was simply a bizarre sight and probably not one that the authorities would approve of.

There is always another side to disappointment and driving away from Bromsgrove the spirits were lifted when news came through that fierce rivals Farnborough Town, whose fans had promised, among other things, that they would do much better than The Cards, had been relegated. Relegation of course was to become a fairly regular fact of life for them as they 'enjoyed' a yo-yo relationship with the top tier and the pyramid over the years.

As for the Woking season, it said it all that Senior was the leading marksman with just 13 goals to his credit. His striking partner Puckett managed 12 but nobody else was capable of scoring more than 6. Batty, who had attained cult status during the 1991/92 Championship season, won England international honours when he played against Finland, a game held at Kingfield, and in another against The Highland League. In doing so, he became the first Woking player to win international recognition for more than 30 years.

Kevan Brown, who had an uncertain start as a full-back and was dropped from the side, knuckled down to the challenge and was voted Player of the Year. He had switched to the centre of the defence and played as though he had been there for his entire career. His immaculate timing and presence won him many admirers and his superb manner made him a great ambassador for Woking. Not many players at any club will ever be held in such high esteem and his memorable Kingfield career was only just beginning.

So, Conference survival had been achieved with something to spare. Chapple's men had gained 59 points from 42 matches to finish in eighth position – but only 11 points off the bottom three. They had scored 58 goals but had also let in 62.

The obvious clamour and desire to sample football at the top level of non-League football was understandable and widespread but the standard of play of a large number of teams was neither entertaining nor adventurous. Far too many sides simply relied on launching the ball forward, with big forwards bearing down on balls knocked towards them by equally large defenders. It was clear that although Chapple had done his level best to recruit suitable players, there was a need to inject more steel into the side and augment what skill there was with yet more. Easier said than done of course, but the important point was that he at least had the opportunity to do so when, for quite some time, the side looked to have the potential for being the Conference's unwanted answer to one-hit wonders from the world of pop music.

2

One for the Trophy Cabinet
1993/94

The fact that Woking entered season number two in non-League's elite meant that they had survived their biggest test, that of retaining their Conference status. There had been a number of doubters throughout the first season in the top flight and the experts all warned that the real test would come in the second season. His players had done him proud, but in customary Geoff Chapple style, there was a significant amount of player movement during the summer. Out went Richard Nugent, Mark Fleming, Trevor Senior, Robbie Carroll and Ansil Bushay, who had looked the business up front but did not get as much of a chance to shine as a number of other players over the years.

Joining the club were Gwynne Berry (once of Sutton United), Mark Tucker (formerly with Fulham), Reuben Agboola (who had played at the highest level with Southampton) and a certain player by the name of Clive Walker. Not too many people seriously believed, after seeing Walker in a pre-season friendly, that he would actually be joining the club but join he did. Agboola had a very good pedigree but he had dropped out of top-flight football after injury and it was not long before he left on account of his recurring problems.

The season started with a 0-0 draw away to Northwich Victoria and although nobody would have thought of the long-term benefit when Dave Puckett missed a spot kick, his failure to score meant that penalties then became the responsibility of Walker. Having missed what was probably the most important penalty of his career – for Sunderland against Norwich City in the 1985 League Cup Final at Wembley – what a reliable man from 12 yards he turned out to be for Woking.

After the opening match Chapple went into print to say how pleased he was with the new faces and was quoted in the programme for the home match against Welling United as saying: "Each of the five debutants performed with credit, with Reuben Agboola and Mark Tucker gelling well with the superb Kevan Brown, giving the defence a stability we haven't seen for over a year." Unfortunately, by the end of the evening that instability had returned, with Welling taking the three points after a comfortable 2-0 win. Chapple's opinion of Ollie Morah was not known – the former Tottenham Hotspur and Sutton United forward left the club with just one appearance to his credit and had departed Kingfield before Welling breezed into town.

Despite the presence of the new faces, not because of them, the start to the season was just about as dismal as could be. Chapple, forever one to bring in players when he needed to, wasted no time and after just two fixtures signed Lennie Dennis, a player

Dereck Brown receives the 1992/93 Woking Player of the Year award.

who had played in the World Cup for Jamaica. Dennis had an excellent record of scoring in non-League football, principally with Sutton and Welling.

The slow start got worse, with humiliation in a crushing 5-0 defeat by newly promoted Dover Athletic making it a very bleak Bank Holiday Monday drive home from the Channel port. The sight of a managerial legend such as Chapple having to walk through a line of cat-calling fans did nothing to suggest that harmony would soon be restored.

Stafford Rangers ran out comfortable 3-0 winners when the sides met in The Potteries and after five matches only one goal had been scored in the process of picking up two points, meaning the team was now nestling in twenty-first place.

By the time Macclesfield Town arrived at Kingfield in the second week of September, for what was the sixth fixture of the season, Chapple had not started consecutive games with the same eleven players. However, the side that he plumped for that afternoon certainly did the business for him and a 3-0 win lifted the team to sixteenth place. In goal for Macclesfield that day was Steve Farrelly, later to play under Chapple at both Kingstonian and Woking. Farrelly saw red when he was quite rightly dismissed for violent conduct – hitting Keiron Swift as Walker prepared to take a corner. Quite how the referee subsequently awarded a penalty when the ball was not in play remains a mystery but nobody was going to look a gift horse in the mouth and Walker slotted home the first spot kick of his Woking career – part of a brace for him that afternoon.

Striker Peter Heritage, once of Hereford United, was the next, somewhat surprising, signing and he made his debut in a 0-0 draw away to Bromsgrove Rovers. Heritage only

Lennie Dennis chalks up another goal.

made two more appearances before departing without a goal to his credit. Things had looked a bit brighter after the fixture in Worcestershire but seven days later there was a massive injection of reality as Halifax Town cruised to a thumping 6-2 win at Kingfield. Perhaps they had been inspired by Chapple when he wrote beforehand:

The Shaymen certainly haven't found their start to Conference life easy and they start today's game still looking for their first win. But, as I have said before, the Conference is a unique competition and once the club has had a chance to settle, and with the luxury of a full-time squad, I'm sure they'll soon start to climb up the table.

How very prophetic those words were, especially as he also waxed lyrical about The Cards having solved their defensive problems, having kept two clean sheets.

In the light of that crushing defeat, Chapple warned that he would be "scouring the land for players from the lower leagues in the hope of uncovering a gem who will not cost us a fortune". Kevin Rattray, who was one such rare stone, scored his first goal for the club and with Walker scoring his fourth in four games, three extremely useful and necessary points were picked up as Merthyr Tydfil were sent packing on the back of a 2-1 defeat.

Chapple then introduced another loan signing. He was a striker and had a famous goalscorer's name, albeit with a lower profile than his more prestigious namesake. Andy Gray made his debut at Southport but his goal was not enough to gain so much as a point.

But there was a chink in the gloom. Dover came to Kingfield on a night of pouring rain and on the waterlogged Kingfield pitch, revenge for the Bank Holiday debacle was gained with a 3-0 win over the league leaders. That match was pivotal and sparked a fourteen-game unbeaten run.

In the first week of October Chapple introduced Jody Craddock, a youngster on his way to what later turned out to be Premiership football with Sunderland. He, as was the case with another signing later in the season, was recruited on loan from Cambridge United. Witton Albion were brushed aside 3-1 at Kingfield, with Craddock scoring his first goal for the club and there followed a spirited revival away to Halifax, with the team recovering from a two goal deficit to win 3-2. Anybody with an eye for an outside bet on the scorers in that game would have won a few bob with the unlikely pairing of Tucker and Andy Clement finding the target.

After sharing the points against Telford United, in a 0-0 draw, there was a break from Conference action. Welling United, yet again, put paid to any hopes (were there actually any?) of making progress in the Bob Lord Trophy. The Wings certainly had the Indian sign over Woking and their tactics did not impress Chapple. "Welling's long ball tactics certainly were very frustrating and if you want to get a headache Park View Road is certainly the place to go," he said. "I suppose, to be honest, Welling just about deserved their win but I'll rue the day should a Woking side ever have to resort to those tactics". Well those days would certainly come in a later era. Dennis, of course, had previously been on the end of many long balls at Welling and caused damage to Woking a number of times, but Chapple had not been slow to sign him and what a good, honest signing he was too.

FA Cup action was then the start of a packed period of matches. On the face of it a home tie against Weston-Super-Mare in the famous old competition should not have

The legendary Clive Walker gets in a cross against Bromsgrove Rovers.

been too difficult, but with the game ending 2-2 the replay was certainly not going to be easy. In the league another point was gained in a 2-2 draw away to Stalybridge Celtic, the highlight of which was a superb goal by Craddock. The club then hosted the visit of Kidderminster Harriers, the team destined to win the title but be denied their place in the Football League because of ground requirements. Walker, with his eighth goal of the season, ensured Woking took all three points.

The midweek FA Cup replay in Somerset was duly won 1-0, thanks to another goal from Clement, but blizzard conditions made it impossible for a number of Woking fans to get to the ground before half-time. As so often happens in cup competitions, the matches come immediately before or after league meetings between the two clubs and a week after beating Kidderminster Harriers 1-0 at Kingfield, the pair met at Aggborough in the second round of the FA Cup. Revenge was sweet for the Worcestershire outfit as they meted out a 1-0 defeat to Chapple's side, before going on to eventually face West Ham United and their own departure from the competition.

From that point on it was Conference football through to the third week of January, with three wins and four draws coming from games against Bath City, who had defeated Hereford United – at that time a Football League club – Gateshead, Slough Town, Welling United, Kettering Town, Altrincham and Macclesfield Town. And then, in the unlikely setting of the New Forest, one of the great cup records of modern days was born. In close proximity to ponies, donkeys and asses, Woking faced Bashley in the FA Trophy and got through an awkward tie with something to spare. A brace from Dennis made it five goals in three outings for him. It was Shane Wye's last game before he returned to New Zealand and so it was fitting that he should score after the home side had taken the lead.

Inspired by the win down among the trees and wildlife, Woking managed to record a 1-0 home win over Southport before losing 2-0 away to Telford United. It was then back to FA Trophy action, with an away tie against Dagenham & Redbridge – a far more daunting task than the previous round. However, a superb performance encouraged some to dream of walking up Wembley Way and saw Ladbrokes install Woking as 9/2 favourites to win at Wembley, despite a reality check when the previous season's league runners-up Bromsgrove Rovers were paired with The Cards in the third round. Having failed to beat them in three Conference meetings since 1992, the Woking fans had every reason to fear that the Wembley dream would end here. While waiting for the clash, league matches saw a 3-0 defeat away to Kettering Town, the side beaten with some ease. Things then got back on track with a 3-0 home win against Stalybridge Celtic.

Nerves were tested at Kingfield in the Trophy tie. Bromsgrove, with three England non-League internationals in their side, twice took the lead but Barry Lakin, probably Woking's forgotten man in what turned out to be a fabulous season, scored the decisive goal in The Cards' 3-2 win. The game was also memorable for a spectacular diving header from Kevan Brown in front of the Kingfield Road End. Brown didn't score many goals but when he did he did so in style.

Dave Puckett, Kevan Brown, Colin Lippiatt and Mark Biggins.

Strangely enough, Chapple did not go into raptures over the game; instead he claimed: "We didn't play to our capabilities and it was not due to tension. The display can be best described as lacklustre." Things often look different from the dugout but the atmosphere had been great and it was end-to-end stuff, with the outcome in doubt virtually to the last kick.

There then followed another excellent clash at Dagenham. Although Woking were on top for virtually the entire 90 minutes, the 4-3 win that Chapple's men secured was far too close for comfort – not that the boss saw the game, as he had fallen victim to a bout of influenza. Nevertheless, it was great stuff and the Woking fans made the most of a good day with plenty of good-hearted banter throughout.

Only two points were picked up over the course of the next three matches, with draws against Altrincham and Bromsgrove being followed by a 3-1 defeat at Kidderminster. Woking's goal that afternoon was scored by a player who had sampled Conference and FA Trophy success with Colchester United, but Gary Bennett's stay at Kingfield was short lived – presumably he was not considered to be one of the gems that Chapple had scoured the country for.

Merthyr Tydfil, on another soaking wet evening, lost 3-2 to The Cards in a midweek fixture before the footballing public of Woking were introduced to a new name. Billingham Synthonia, sounding more like a brass band than a football team, arrived for the FA Trophy fourth-round fixture. The club, born out of being the ICI works team up on Teeside, arrived at Kingfield having claimed the Conference scalps of Kettering and Macclesfield in the competition and Gateshead in the FA Cup. In line with those achievements, Billingham took the lead and resolute defending looked like succeeding until Walker made it 1-1.

The hardy Woking fans set off for the midweek replay. They saw their team once again fall behind but on hand was the elegant Brown, in amongst the goals again. His two, great, wind-assisted strikes were enough for Woking to qualify for the semi-final stage. Fans and players arrived back home just about in time to get washed and ready for work the next morning but nobody seemed to be too bothered about that minor inconvenience.

Over the Easter period a 1-0 win was achieved at home to Gateshead and two days later Chapple introduced a young striker by the name of Darran Hay. He, like Craddock, came to the club on loan from Cambridge United. His debut away to Slough Town was an unremarkable affair and ended 0-0, but 4 April 1994 was the start of something special. Hay was to become inexorably linked to success and Woking. His first goal came in a 2-1 defeat away to Runcorn and he scored the winner at Bath five days later, largely due it has to be said to a lineswoman who somehow missed the fact that he was offside by a considerable distance.

Only four days later just under 4,000 fans flocked to Kingfield to watch the FA Trophy semi-final first leg against Enfield. This marked the first time that The Cards had reached the semi-final stage since being eliminated by Dagenham in 1979/80. An important member of the visiting side was the former Tottenham Hotspur, Glasgow Rangers and England defender Graham Roberts, the player-manager of the side. He, of course, was surely expecting some stick, having been in the West Brom team humbled by Tim Buzaglo and Co in the FA Cup a few years earlier. Whatever sentiments Roberts may have had about the welcome he received only got worse when he scored an own goal to put Woking ahead. However, the tense clash ended 1-1 and the question of whether Woking had the steel to win in North London was asked.

Before travelling to find out there was a midweek Conference fixture to be played, Dagenham, who Woking had beaten 2-1 and 4-3 in recent weeks, were the visitors and surely nobody could have expected the way that events turned out. Chapple, in his programme notes, eulogised over how entertaining the two previous clashes between the clubs had been that season. One wonders whether he was as generous with his words to his players at the end of the evening. Woking had their chances and at half-time there was nothing in it. Hay scored again, but then the world went crazy. Woking crashed 8-1 in what remains the second heaviest home defeat in the history of Conference football. The whole scene was like something out of bad dream and the nightmare thought was that in less than 128 hours there was the small matter of a trip to Enfield.

Despite the seismic defeat during the week, the players showed they had the resolve in the second leg at Enfield and held out for a 0-0 draw after extra-time. Three days later it was a trip to Adams Park, the home of Wycombe Wanderers, for the replay. Hay, with a brace, plus another from Scott Steele, confirmed a place in the Trophy final with an emphatic 3-0 win.

Enfield's Graham Roberts puts through his own net in the FA Trophy at Kingfield.

There were still five Conference meetings to fulfil before anybody could start to think too deeply about Wembley and quite how the players managed to cope with a fixture list that would never be contemplated by a Premiership club is anyone's guess. Those five games were fitted in during the space of a week. On the Saturday the team gained a point with a 0-0 draw away to Witton Albion, and, courtesy of the *Daily Mirror*, the faces of the Wembley finalists were shown, in colour, to the nation. Sunday was a day off from football but on the Monday evening there was a trip down the A303 to Yeovil where, by virtue of an own goal and a missed penalty, The Cards picked up three valuable points – The Glovers remaining in fear of relegation.

There were no fixtures on the Tuesday and Wednesday, but on the Thursday evening Yeovil gained revenge with a 2-1 win. The following evening only 692 footy-fatigued fans – Woking's lowest ever Conference gate at Kingfield – made the effort to watch what must have been a very tired side beat Northwich Victoria 2-1. The Conference season was rounded off with the visit of Stafford Rangers, when an emphatic 4-0 win capped a hectic week, sending home fans away full of expectation for the visit, fourteen days later, to Wembley.

The players had shown tremendous resolve and a finishing spot of third in the Conference was richly deserved. The Surrey Senior Cup was secured at the Kingsmeadow home of Kingstonian, with a comfortable 3-0 win over Sutton United. Who, at that stage, would have linked Chapple, Kingstonian and cup success? Runcorn had prevailed in the other FA Trophy semi-final and, worryingly, they had taken four points off The Cards in Conference clashes during the season.

'Ooh Darran Hay' in FA Trophy action.

On FA Trophy final day itself the heavens opened, saturating the Wembley pitch to the extent that it was questionable as to whether or not the game could go ahead. The conditions were farcical, with massive puddles halting the progress of the ball and players kicking up huge plumes of water every time they swung their feet or tried to run with it. Hay had, in a very short spell, become a hero but it was Dereck Brown, a man respected by everyone, who put Woking ahead early on. Hay added a second and Woking looked, quite appropriately given the conditions, to be cruising.

But there were fears when, in what must rank as a unique event in cup final history, both Brown and Hay were injured and had to be substituted, neither appearing after half-time.

Despite the side having to be reorganised, Runcorn simply could not break them down, although Woking hearts were tested when Gwynne Berry conceded a 74th-minute penalty. The celebrations following a famous triumph were, not unnaturally, fairly flamboyant and every player took his turn at diving across the famous surface. This had been an incredible season after an awful start. To have finished third in the Conference was nothing short of remarkable given the number of fixtures that had to be fitted in as the season drew to a close. To lift the Surrey Senior Cup, especially against old rivals Sutton United, was another night to remember but it all took second place to the Wembley victory.

For many people, however, there was a tinge of sadness about it all. Hay, after all, had only been on loan and the final was possibly going to be his last game for the club. As well as bringing his talent onto the pitch and scoring that afternoon, he had his own Caribbean band of followers, along with their drums and other assorted instruments,

Scott Steele works his magic against Stalybridge Celtic.

planted in among the Woking faithful. They created a carnival atmosphere all afternoon and who cared about getting wet? Certainly not too many people from Woking that much is certain. There was a funny side, too, as Hay had to find his own way back from the stadium – the team coach having left without him, thinking he had made other arrangements.

Looking back on the season Walker, who had started in a midfield role, had been redeployed as a striker and his partnership with Dennis paid dividends. Tucker, who had been with Fulham, did not enjoy the best of starts with the club and soon fell from favour. However, the end of Craddock's loan spell and the absence through injury of Clement opened the door for him and he underwent a remarkable transformation, becoming a lynchpin in what became a formidable defence.

In fairness to Chapple, his preference for experience served him well and Walker revelled in the role he had been given. It was rumoured that Chapple and Walker didn't see eye to eye on things but there can be no doubt that their combined talents were a massive hit with the fans. Walker had a certain arrogance about him but he had every right, with his sublime skills proving too much for most teams. His class shone through and there can be very few players who have made such an impression at Conference level in his first season in the non-League arena.

Walker was so often the catalyst during games and he developed a fantastic understanding with Steele. With his ability to put the ball on a plate, Walker was

Clive Walker directs the Weston-Super-Mare defence.

the perfect man to supply the likes of Hay and Dennis. In addition to laying on countless opportunities and goals for those around him, he weighed in with 23 of his own from 52 appearances. Chapple's boldness in signing Walker had been questioned by some and there were those who felt that the former Chelsea star was simply looking for an easy time of it all. Nothing could have been further from the truth, with the bald-headed maestro turning in breathtaking performances time after time.

For the genial Chapple, the Wembley win represented another significant entry on his record of achievements. The season had comprised 59 matches and Kevan Brown, an inspirational captain, missed just one of them. His namesake, Dereck, won England non-League international caps and deservedly so. Rattray was a revelation, with his transformation from park football to hitting the bar as a second-half substitute at Wembley. His stamina seemingly knew no bounds and although he was not the most elegant of midfielders, his overall ability coupled with his enthusiasm made him a key member of the side.

There is always a sad side to cup success and the sympathy vote simply had to go to Dennis. He had won over the fans and more than contributed to a great season. However, he ended the campaign empty handed after a broken jaw consigned him to the sidelines for the closing two months.

The signing of Hay was another masterstroke by Chapple and Lippiatt. He scored vital goals and his presence was even more crucial given the absence of Dennis. A strike

Boing, Boing, Woking, Woking – FA Trophy Final *v.* Runcorn.

Lloyd Wye and Andy Clement celebrate the 1994 FA Trophy win in Town Square with boss Geoff Chapple.

rate of 8 goals in 13 games had the Woking fans clamouring for the club to sign him on a permanent basis, but his success at Woking meant that Cambridge United were unlikely to agree to let him go – at least for the time being.

The whole town celebrated the success – something that was long overdue after the FA Amateur Cup triumph way back in 1958. There was an open-top bus ride throughout the Borough, and receptions and autograph signing sessions in Woking Park. It had been a difficult road to Wembley and the journey looked, on several occasions, to be over. Chapple, always the one with a line for the press, wondered what was next on the agenda. He had a keen appetite for success and his association with the FA Trophy and Wembley had only just begun. The big question was whether or not he could bring about more success and in what form would it come?

Despite the win at Wembley, the club was hardly in the best of health financially and for Chapple there was not going to be masses of cash with which to strengthen what had become a fairly formidable squad, albeit one that lacked real strength in depth. Chapple himself, at the celebration dinner given in honour of the Wembley triumph, said: "What can one achieve now?" The answer was not too far away and very few people could have been disappointed by the encore to the Lord Mayor's Show.

3
Let the Good Times Roll
1994/95

With the Lord Mayor's Show over and done with the previous season – thanks to a first Wembley triumph for thirty-six years – there was an obvious air of expectancy among the fans that this season could be as good, if not better. Having tasted the experience of a Wembley visit and basked in the glory of winning underneath the Twin Towers, nobody could have expected a return trip twelve months later. And yet, incredibly, it was about to happen once again and while nobody knew it at the time, the club was carving out a niche for itself in the annals of history.

During the summer Geoff Chapple released Andy Clement and Dave Puckett, two of his most experienced but reportedly high-earning players. Another departure was the legendary Mark Biggins. In 292 appearances 'Biggo' had scored 44 goals, but an injury sustained in a cynical challenge at Gateshead in January 1993 severely restricted his subsequent Conference appearances and he eventually ended his Woking days by going on loan to Walton & Hersham. Biggins, a painter and decorator by trade, is still talked about more than a decade on and the memory of him emerging from his van in the club car park, covered in paint, before bemusing the opposition with his impish skills remains legendary. Lee Tierling was a summer recruit, brought into the side in place of Clement after he was released by Fulham.

Awards were no stranger to Clive Walker and as he had been a class apart from most other Conference players the previous season it was no surprise that he received the Woking FC Player of the Year award for 1993/94 prior to kick-off in a pre-season friendly against one of his former clubs, Brighton & Hove Albion. Fittingly, the presentation was made by Liam Brady, one of the most cultured players of his or any other era. Much to the delight of everybody at Kingfield, Darran Hay was back in the fold, having been signed on loan for a second spell from Cambridge United. And so to the start of what would prove to be another historic campaign for The Cards.

Woking had never won on the opening day of a Conference season and Chapple was moved to write in his programme notes, for the visit of Halifax Town: "After the tremendous success of last season everyone is asking what my aims are for the coming nine months. Well, firstly to win some matches at the beginning of the season for a change." That hopeful note soon went flat after The Shaymen, despite being reduced to ten men, strolled to a 3-1 win.

Chapple had also stressed the importance of clubs relying on younger players and home-grown talent. Looking back at the team-sheet for that afternoon, Lloyd Wye could at least be pigeonholed in the latter category, being local and a product of the club. But the fact that he was the only one out of the thirteen named on the day

Colin Fielder – 'Mr Nice Guy'.

showed the reality of the situation. Chapple's aspirations for his team were admirable but youth was not a feature of this present crop of players.

Chapple was cautious when looking ahead to what might be achieved after the euphoria that enveloped the previous season. The manager went into print saying:

Not wishing to be too negative, my main aim this season is to retain the club's Conference status. Even though the bookies have us as third favourites to win the title, strength in depth is what is needed to win this competition and that is something that we just haven't got.

Programme editor Mike Deavin was far more positive when he predicted a top-three finish. He also touched on the subject of budgets, a theme that has been inexorably linked with Woking over the years. Deavin's editorial focused on goalkeepers who had become managers and he concluded that Laurence Batty may have more sense than to follow the example of the likes of Peter Shilton and Ray Clemence. But time would show that Batty was not in any way put off with the disappointing experiences of those two former greats and in 2002/03 took the plunge at Ryman Division One side Walton & Hersham.

The season was off and running and, inspired by Hay, there were consecutive 2-1 victories over Welling United and Altrincham, who had been topping the table. A Bank Holiday Monday home fixture against Merthyr Tydfil saw history made when Hay notched the first ever Woking hat-trick in the Conference in a convincing 4-1 win that left the club in third place at the end of the afternoon.

Telford United were greeted a few days later and a brace from Kevin Rattray secured the third 2-1 win in four games. Stevenage Borough were new to the Conference at that time and a Monday evening fixture at their Broadhall Way ground was settled when Walker scored the only goal of the game. Halcyon days indeed because, on Monday 5 September 1994, the club had climbed to the highest ever position in its 105-year history – top of the Conference. Considering the reservations that Chapple had in terms of the strength of his squad, the top spot had been reached after six games and with only twelve players used. Was it a case of quality rather than quantity?

Stafford Rangers had failed to pick up a point after six matches and were three points adrift at the foot of the table when they arrived at Kingfield for The Cards' seventh fixture. Having had five straight victories, there was a bit of a reality check for Woking when the strugglers took a point in a 2-2 draw. For Hay, things were going from good to excellent, with a brace taking him to six goals from the opening seven starts. While it was all wonderful stuff from the Woking point of view, the fear remained that Cambridge United would want Hay back and reap the benefits of the form their young striker was showing.

Yeovil Town, another club that were down towards the foot of the table, also took a point in a 2-2 draw at Kingfield. It goes without saying that Hay again found the back of their net. The poor results continued at Runcorn and a 1-0 defeat meant that the club slipped from their heady heights to fifth place. By virtue of winning the FA Trophy, the club then played Kidderminster Harriers in the Championship Shield. Chapple introduced new blood in midfield and in Andy Ellis, who made his debut, he had picked up somebody who proved a real gem. Few people had ever heard of Ellis, but the man who had played European Cup Winners Cup football with Barry Town was destined to become one of the most popular players the club had signed and he was inexorably linked with good flowing football and success in red and white halves.

Grant Payne celebrates his goal at Stevenage in the 3-0 FA Trophy win.

Payney's mates join in the fun at Broadhall Way.

Chapple, having recruited the Welshman, missed his opening gambit in a Cards shirt as he was suffering from an abscess on a tooth. Colin Lippiatt took charge of the team and Chapple was reduced to receiving updates on the game courtesy of mobile phone conversations with football secretary Phil Ledger. Quite how much pain Chapple felt at the start of the evening is not known. He could not have felt comfortable when he heard that Dereck Brown, for so long the star in Woking's midfield, arrived late at Aggborough, leaving Lippiatt with no choice other than to play Ellis from the outset. It was a great start for both player and acting manager as Kidderminster were beaten 2-1 in front of their own fans. Needless to say, it was Hay who scored both goals.

It was business as usual when, on 24 September 1994, Southport were the visitors. The date marked exactly ten years in charge for Chapple and in that time he had transformed a sleeping giant into a club that was slogging it out at the top of the non-League tree. He had overseen three promotions and six cup final wins, not to mention some incredible cup runs that had launched the club onto the front, as well as the back pages of the national press. The Southport matchday programme was largely a celebration of the Chapple years and his players added to the party atmosphere with a 3-0 win over the former Football League outfit.

Bath City then became the third side to leave Kingfield on the back of a 2-2 draw, after Terry Molloy, a trustee of the club and member of the management committee, used the Bath programme to air his views on the possible relocation of the club – a subject that had been mooted – saying:

Marlow – Sunday FA Cup winners as the Cards crash out in the first round.

...we are seeking relocation where the developer would provide us with an acceptable stadium. Progress on relocation is slow because of the reluctance of councillors to agree to a site. As soon as there is something to report on relocation you will be informed because it is accepted that all our fans and supporters are thirsting for information.

After detailing how supporters could help in securing the 'new stadium', Molloy then concluded by adding: "Let us now all be positive and launch a campaign to bring League football to Woking and not be satisfied until that end has been achieved."

Gateshead, who had a large stadium with very few fans in it, became the third side to beat Woking, their 2-0 win the second consecutive Conference away match to end in defeat. But Hay, with a brace, and Lennie Dennis proved too much for Kettering Town in a 3-1 win in front of 2,277 – up until that point The Cards' biggest home crowd of the season. Hay had taken his goal tally to 13 and although Chapple may have been aware of the fact, few Woking fans knew that the goalscoring machine had made his last home appearance of his loan spell. After lining up in the side that won 2-1 away to Yeovil Town in the following fixture, Hay was summoned back to the Abbey Stadium, having helped Woking through the 150-point barrier in their short Conference history. Chapple waxed lyrical about the departed Hay, saying: "I am sure we will all follow his league career with interest".

With the in-form striker back with his employers, Ellis was also missing from the side that faced Northwich Victoria. He was busy signing an important contract elsewhere as he got married. The Northwich game was the 100th that Woking played in the Conference but there was not a great deal to celebrate at the end of another home draw. What was worth noting was the fact that over the previous 99 matches, Chapple's side had secured more points than any other club taking part in the 1994/95 campaign.

Dennis, in the absence of Hay, proved his value to the side. The Jamaican international scored twice in the 2-0 home win against Runcorn that took the club back to top spot. The following week he grabbed another brace in a 3-2 victory away to Stafford Rangers. As a replacement for Hay, Chapple could not have wished for more.

Into November and The Bob Lord Trophy never really caught the imagination – a 0-0 draw at home to Farnborough Town did little to endear it to the faithful. In reality it was precisely the outcome that neither club wanted at the onset of winter and the inevitable fixture congestion that ensues. As Farnborough departed, Kidderminster Harriers dropped in for a Conference clash, but just like the Hampshire outfit before them they were unable to find the net. Worse still, neither could Woking.

In an amazing FA Cup first-round tie at Underhill, Woking drew 4-4 with Barnet. Unbelievably, Chapple's side had stormed into a 3-0 lead before half-time but the Football League outfit, just as Woking had done in the opening 45 minutes, made the most of their famous slope and pulled back two goals. Woking scored again through Walker to give themselves a two-goal cushion but Barnet were not done and levelled it up in the eight-goal thriller. It was only the third time in ten years that a non-League club had scored four times on a Football League ground. Sutton United had done it at Colchester and a Tim Buzaglo-inspired Woking did it at West Bromwich Albion. Sadly it later transpired that a tragedy had occurred during the afternoon as Harry Pullen, a longstanding and loyal supporter of The Cards, had collapsed and died during the interval. He had been one of the 87 originals who had witnessed Chapple's first game in charge in 1984 against Clapton. It was a sad event and somewhat flew in the face of the statement, made by the late Bill Shankly, that football was more important than life itself.

Chapple considered the first-half performance the best he had seen in ten years as manager, although he accepted that a draw was a fair result. The replay was settled by a solitary Mark Tucker goal and the reward was a second-round tie away to Marlow – a match which was not destined to go according to plan as far as The Cards were concerned.

Stalybridge Celtic, at their Bower Fold ground that nestles in the hills outside Manchester, won 2-1 in the Conference in late November, the consolation for Woking being that the goal from Dennis was their 150th in the top flight of the non-League game. Rattray's strike settled the Bob Lord Trophy replay at Farnborough, recording Woking's first win in the competition after three seasons of trying, although it has to be said that the word trying could be loosely applied to some of the performances in what was realistically the Conference league cup.

The FA Cup, however, brings about its own anticipation, especially at the second-round stage where dreams of a trip to Old Trafford or Anfield surface. Some thought that the

Kevin Rattray in the heat of the midfield battle.

trip to Buckinghamshire to face Marlow would be little more than a formality against a team from the Isthmian League.

What Woking fans had overlooked about their opponents when the second-round draw was made, was that the Bucks' side had also beaten Football League opposition in the form of Oxford United. On a heavy pitch at The Alfred Davis Memorial Ground, hardly conducive to the free-flowing football Woking were used to conjuring up, the chance of a money-spinning third-round tie was destined to pass the club by. Despite the fourteen-man squad that Chapple named containing thirteen of the players that had a part to play in the defeat of Barnet, things just did not go the way that many anticipated. Marlow's winning goal came in the 90th minute and a 2-1 victory was nothing less than the home side deserved. Chapple went on to describe the afternoon as, "the blackest day of my career to date and all the team were as sick as pigs".

Macclesfield Town had enjoyed a good run of results and their 2-0 home win over Woking in the Conference left them nine points clear of The Cards with half the season gone. Cup football was back on the agenda when the Metropolitan Police were easily defeated in the Surrey Senior Cup ahead of a home game against Bromsgrove Rovers. Dave Greene, who had scored two in the 3-0 win over the boys in blue, followed that up with both goals in the 2-0 triumph over Bromsgrove in the last Conference fixture before Christmas. Before the festivities there was time to lose 2-1 away to Kettering Town in the Bob Lord Trophy, although no tears were shed at being removed from that particular competition.

Another firm favourite, Dereck Brown, had left the club and signed for Walton & Hersham (after more than 200 appearances to his credit) by the time Woking hosted

Lloyd Wye is first to congratulate Clive Walker after the winger's FA Trophy penalty winner at Macclesfield Town.

Dagenham & Redbridge. In his programme notes Chapple was spot on when he said: "The games between us are usually full of goals (a total of 16 from the two Conference games last season) so let's hope the players put on a good, entertaining show today".

With The Cards scoring three but losing in an eight-goal thriller, it was certainly entertaining, but less so from the Woking point of view, especially as the Londoners were struggling to avoid dropping into the relegation places. After a draw at Merthyr, during which Laurence Batty was sent off, and a revenge 2-0 win at Dagenham, the next stop was Bromsgrove.

Chapple introduced another new name, having signed Grant Payne on loan from Wimbledon. The newcomer must have wondered what on earth Conference football was all about. In no time at all Woking were trailing by two goals and an amazing match finished 5-5. Payne had scored on his debut for the club, something that was to become a habit for him.

Before the forthcoming FA Trophy first-round tie with Chesham, Ted Hills, the club chairman, penned a plea in the programme, taking the opportunity to comment on those who were perhaps too satisfied with the way things were going at Kingfield. "This self admiration is fine, but where do we go from here?" he said. "The answer must be forward to the Football League. If not, there is a great danger of a drift backwards, which has been the case in the past for other clubs. This must not be allowed to happen at Woking." Hills concluded by adding:

The hills are steep, but we can climb these with better communications and commitment. With a unity of aims our objectives can be reached. Through the programme, newsletters, bulletins, local press and radio we can strengthen our defence, increase our striking power and make those goals that matter as much off the pitch as on. As a club we must all strive to go forward and work together to build a future for Woking FC.

There was no mention of seagulls and trawlers but the prophecy certainly had a touch of the Cantona about it. Whatever he meant, it was hardly a clear explanation of how Woking could make progress. In the match itself, the club's first defence of the Trophy they had gloriously won the previous season, Ellis scored his first goal for the club, with Scott Steele and Walker also getting in on the act in a straightforward 3-0 win that set up a home tie against Cheltenham Town in the next round.

After an emphatic 4-0 defeat away to Halifax Town, which Chapple missed on account of a bout of food poisoning, The Cards travelled to Alwyns Lane to face Chertsey Town in the Surrey Senior Cup. In what the manager must surely have regarded as an even blacker day than the defeat at Marlow, a near full-strength Woking crashed to a humiliating 6-1 hammering to relinquish their hold on a trophy they picked up when beating Sutton United the previous season. With only four days to go until welcoming Cheltenham to Kingfield for the latest Trophy instalment, Chapple's charges had conceded ten goals in the space of 180 minutes.

Woking players celebrate the tremendous cup win at Macclesfield Town.

Only Scarborough had ever retained the FA Trophy, but a return to form at Kingfield saw that particular dream live on for the club, with the visitors journeying back to Gloucestershire on the back of a 3-1 defeat. The next fixture was more than two weeks later in March – the third-round Trophy tie at Stevenage. It was fast becoming the toughest of all routes to the final. Steele and Walker scored in a 3-0 win and the game was notable for former Woking defender Richard Nugent being sent off after incidents involving Rattray and Shane Wye. One week later the clubs met at Kingfield in a Conference encounter and there was a repeat 3-0 win for Woking. The historic rivalry between the two clubs was beginning to form with a vengeance.

The game marked the arrival of John Crumplin, a former Brighton & Hove Albion team-mate of Walker, signed on a match-by-match basis. Chapple made the most of the signing, saying:

John has been released by Brighton after more than 200 appearances. He is still only twenty-seven and a class performer. Unfortunately, due to the club's financial position, I'm not sure how long we'll be able to keep him, but he could prove to be a tremendous asset for us and a worthwhile investment. Still, we have to see if the necessary funds will be made available.

Chapple had cleverly used his programme notes, ensuring that his wishes would be made public and a certain amount of pressure applied to the management committee.

After a 0-0 draw at home to Dover Athletic, there was a run of four away games. Kidderminster Harriers were beaten 3-1, a result that registered Woking's 50th Conference win, and a 0-0 draw was achieved against Telford United. It was then back

Kevin Rattray gets buried under team-mates at Kingfield after his semi-final goal against Rushden & Diamonds in the FA Trophy.

to FA Trophy action and a game that would surely have graced Wembley itself. Macclesfield Town were racing away at the top of the Conference and were clear favourites to progress to the semi-final stage. In a marvellous game it was a tale of two penalties. Walker, in customary style, tucked his away but Macclesfield wasted their opportunity from 12 yards. With Ellis unavailable due to suspension, Chapple had been forced to make changes but nobody could have found fault with a performance that defied the odds and put the club within touching distance of Wembley for the second time in the space of a year.

After a great run of results Chapple was named as the *Mail on Sunday* Manager of the Month for March. It was the first time he had picked up the award and he did so after his side had gone through the month undefeated, conceding just one goal and scoring ten in six games.

On April Fool's Day Woking travelled to Northwich and gained a point in a 2-2 draw. Chapple subsequently criticised the players for not having their minds on the game, after the loss of two more points that should have been theirs. More significantly, the game marked the return of Hay to Cambridge United, but his trip back to the Abbey Stadium did not work out as well as he may have hoped and it was not long before he was back at Kingfield. This time it was on a permanent basis, with a reported £15,000 being exchanged between the two parties.

Farnborough Town lost 3-2 at Kingfield just a few days before Chapple's side lined up at Nene Park to face Rushden & Diamonds in the FA Trophy semi-final first leg. Outside of Northamptonshire few people had heard of the Beazer Homes League side. With the financial backing of Max Griggs and his Dr Marten's footwear empire, the club had a fantastic stadium and a strong squad. Quite how Woking managed to restrict the margin of defeat to one goal was difficult to understand. Had they taken their chances on the day the fans of the 'minnows' could have booked their Wembley seats there and then. However, the return leg went the way of Woking with goals from Rattray and Walker. Woking had won the right to defend their title and the date of Sunday 14 May was clearly marked on numerous calendars as showing another commitment in north London. In the other semi-final Kidderminster Harriers got the better of Hyde United, so the opposition would be familiar. They would also be tough.

Hay had not looked the same player since returning to the club and a run of four games without a goal must have been a worry for Chapple. Hay finally rediscovered his shooting boots when he scored in a 1-1 draw at home to Gateshead and he went on to notch another in a 2-0 victory at Farnborough. Macclesfield arrived at Kingfield with the Conference title as good as in the bag. Once again Walker scored and once again Macclesfield wasted a penalty, with Batty pulling off his third consecutive penalty save. Ahead of that match, Chapple acknowledged in public just how fortunate his side had been in avoiding a heavy defeat at Rushden in the Trophy semi-final, but he was already salivating over what he referred to as 'the friendly final' against Kidderminster.

With a congested fixture list in the build up to Wembley, Chapple took immense pride in the way his team refused to give up the ghost to keep the title race alive. Two points were dropped when Welling United secured a 1-1 draw at Kingfield before Stalybridge

Cards' fans celebrate their Wembley booking.

Colin Fielder heading home the last-gasp winner at Wembley.

Celtic were swept aside 4-1. The final four matches of the Conference season were played in the space of five days, with two wins and two defeats signalling the end of a campaign that left the club in the runner-up spot. Bath City and Southport both secured 2-0 wins in front of their own fans. Dover Athletic lost 3-2 at The Crabble, in a match that took The Cards' aggregate number of Conference points to 200, securing second spot behind Macclesfield in the process. Altrincham were crushed 4-0 at Woking and with the league season ending eight days before the FA Trophy Final, there was concern over the fitness of Crumplin.

Lloyd Wye, not someone who would feign injury and more likely to be the first volunteer if any walls needed walking through, was another doubtful starter after being confined to bed with a stomach upset the day before the final. As it transpired both Crumplin and Wye, who was about to spend his twenty-eighth birthday on the hallowed turf, were declared fit. In front of 17,815 spectators Steele got Woking off to the best possible start when he scored after just 59 seconds, to record one of the fastest ever goals seen at Wembley at any level of the game. It was also a stunner. After turning England non-League international Paul Webb inside out, he then curled a sensational shot over the head of Kevin Rose from all of 25 yards. The conditions could not have been more different from a year earlier against Runcorn. Both sides had their chances and Kidderminster eventually got back on level terms early in the second half. With extra-time virtually over and travel plans for the replay being formulated, it was Colin Fielder who drove a knife through the Kidderminster hearts. His winning goal, courtesy of a firm far-post header, came in the final minute after Mark Tucker had nodded Shane Wye's corner across goal.

It was a never-to-be-forgotten moment for Cards' fans. Tucker must have been the most relieved man on the pitch as a dismissal at Bath would have ruled him out of a replay. Fielder, with the adrenaline pumping, charged the length of the pitch with a trail of Woking players doing their best to keep pace in his slipstream. There was no time left for the Worcestershire outfit to respond and Kevan Brown again led the team up the steps to the Royal Box as winners.

Chapple had mused over what had improved this season. The answer had been provided by a squad of players that provided spectacle after spectacle, with a will to win that gave them a psychological advantage over many opponents. Walker was voted Conference Player of the Year and nobody could argue about the merit of that award. His 25 goals were just part of a huge contribution that he made to the season. For a club that had financial problems and an unwieldy management committee structure that consisted of twelve members, the season had not turned out at all badly. Was it modesty on the part of Chapple when he claimed that survival would be his aim? Did he doubt the ability of his players or himself? Could it possibly have been a case of the larger-than-life manager applying pressure to the twelve controlling men in the public domain? Whatever the strategy may have been, he and Colin Lippiatt had once again overseen a season that for those involved with the club would never be forgotten.

For that the pair of them deserved every accolade they received.

4

Stand and Deliver
1995/96

Basking in another FA Trophy triumph, this was a good time to be a Woking fan. The money was rolling in and everything manager Geoff Chapple touched seemed to turn to gold. It was only hoped that somebody, somewhere, would be ensuring The Cards capitalised on the success that a remarkable group of players had brought to the club. But hindsight was to reveal that this was a long way from reality. For now the committee, management, players and fans were on a roll and matters like putting one over on rivals Stevenage took a good deal of the focus – putting money aside for a rainy day was much lower on the agenda.

During the pre-season matches, Chapple was rewarded with a testimonial against West Ham United. The team's achievements under the leadership of the former postman and insurance salesman had exceeded the wildest dreams of most people, probably even those of Chapple himself. To improve on the previous season was simple to say but not anywhere near as easy to deliver. The fans clamoured for promotion to the Football League and looked to the mercurial Chapple to lead them to the promised land of the full-time game.

The previous season had been close. Would the club ever go so close again? The Conference had been littered with near misses by others and if Woking wanted to succeed there would surely be no place for unnecessarily dropped points, especially at home.

The season proper got underway with a game at the home of reigning champions Macclesfield Town. Chapple had not gone overboard in terms of summer signings but he did bolster the midfield with Carl Hoddle, who was signed from Barnet. It is fair to say that most of the flair in the Hoddle family had rubbed off on Glenn. There was a distinct family likeness in appearance but that is where it ended.

Also recruited into midfield was former England under-21 international Nicky Reid. Both featured in the thirteen players named for the opening fixture but it was an old hand that stole the honours, despite yet another opening-day defeat. Scott Steele scored twice but it was not enough to take anything from the game, with the Cheshire outfit scoring one more. Chapple announced himself satisfied with the display but once again took the opportunity to stress the fact that a large squad was needed in order to progress and that he did not enjoy that luxury.

The first home match of the campaign ended with a 2-0 win over Bath City. Darran Hay got off the mark and Steele scored his third of the season. Losing away to Bromsgrove Rovers a few days later was a bitter pill to swallow as The Cards dominated the match and did not enjoy the rub of the green at all. Much the same could be said of a defeat by the same 2-1 scoreline at Hednesford Town just a few days later. The

Scott Steele and Clive Walker enjoy an arm wrestle.

result sent Woking down to thirteenth in the table with only 6 points from a possible 15, albeit Clive Walker's goal was the 200th The Cards had recorded in Conference football. It was hardly the sort of start that would inspire those dreams of promotion.

Next on the agenda was the visit of Stevenage. Chapple, in his programme notes, praised the Broadhall Way club, saying: "Our guests have made a tremendous start to the season and I favour them for a top-six finish again and they certainly have the potential to actually win the Conference". Was that him being polite, had he consulted a fortune-teller or were Paul Fairclough's side actually good enough to win a strongly contested competition? Whatever the case, there was no doubting which side showed the championship credentials on the night. Stevenage were swept aside in a comfortable 4-1 Woking win, courtesy of goals from Rob Peters, Walker, Reid and Hay. Chapple could hardly contain his enthusiasm in the light of the result. Just four days later he expressed his delight at the way his charges had played and reflected on the fact that as Stevenage were being undone on the pitch, a package had been put together in the local council offices concerning a project which would change the face of Kingfield forever. Woking Borough Council had approved the planning application for a new stand that would enable the club to meet the entry criteria for the Football League. The event inspired the management committee to make a rare statement in the matchday programme, thanking all concerned for their help in progressing the redevelopment. It was a decision that would change the appearance of the ground beyond all recognition and only came about as a result of many hundreds of hours of dedicated and selfless work by a number of people.

Jon Davies, a local businessman and staunch supporter of the club, as well as being a management committee member, gave some background information regarding three years of negotiations leading up to the announcement regarding the ground development. Who at this stage knew that his rise in the ranks of the club would move along parallel lines to that of the Leslie Gosden Stand?

Meanwhile, Halifax Town were beaten 2-0, with Steele coming off the bench to add to his tally of goals. Chapple, who had complained of a lack of strength in depth, had by this time used eighteen players, although only six of them had started every game.

Conference matches away to Kettering Town have always been odd in that only one side has ever scored on the day. Once the home side took the lead, that, on the basis of past history, was that and a 3-0 defeat was no surprise.

However, Colin Fielder and Hay made sure of the points against Runcorn, despite Woking being reduced to ten men after Lloyd Wye was sent off. Once again Woking would contest the Championship Shield. Once again it was there to be won. But, for the second time in the space of a few weeks, Woking left Macclesfield on the back of a 3-2 defeat. That reverse was followed by a 2-0 defeat away to table-topping Kidderminster Harriers, a setback that left The Cards in eighth place and seven points adrift of the leaders.

Off the pitch time was of the essence and, in preparation for building work, the Westfield Terrace was placed out of bounds to spectators. Progress on the stand was fairly rapid and so too was the surge up the table. Chapple's side won six Conference games on the trot following the defeat at Kidderminster. Gateshead, Altrincham and

Darran Hay slides into the box against Morecambe.

Colin Fielder shows style in front of the KRE.

Morecambe were beaten at Kingfield while there were happy away-days at Bath, Welling and Stalybridge. During that period 16 goals were scored, with only one conceded. Steele and Walker made hay with 5 apiece while Hay himself weighed in with 4. Kevan Brown found the target at Welling and Andy Ellis did likewise at Stalybridge, with Walker hitting his first hat-trick for the club. Against Welling, Chapple introduced another new signing and again it was an injection of quality into the side. Steve Thompson had been part of the Wycombe Wanderers side that won the Conference and the FA Trophy. He was supremely fit and went on to form a marvellous midfield partnership with Ellis.

The draw for the FA Cup first round again paired Barnet and Woking and once again the tie was to be played at Underhill. Chapple expressed his disappointment at having to face the Londoners for the second season in a row. He added a few thoughts about the long-term future of Woking when he said: "Our priority must be the Vauxhall Conference and now the ground improvements are underway the pressure on me has increased, but I have broad shoulders and I am always looking to improve our status". Playing against the slope at Barnet the Woking fans had barely settled into the stadium when Hay put The Cards ahead. Ray Clemence, the Barnet manager, had gone public to say that his team must not leave themselves with another mountain to climb after the events of the year before when Woking had raced into a 3-0 lead. Steele added a second after 19 minutes to make the mountain steeper, but two late goals just before half-time left things finely poised for the second half.

Neither side could force an advantage after the break and Barnet were reduced to nine men after moments of madness by Jamie Campbell and Peter Scott. How ironic

Clive Walker fires in a shot against Morecambe.

that the two of them should have Woking connections – Scott having played pre-season games and Campbell destined to become a future Card.

Before the replay, with Enfield or Newport County awaiting the winners, it was off to Slough and the quest for three more league points. They were eventually achieved but not without a few scares along the way. Ansil Bushay, who had not had many opportunities in a Woking shirt, showed Chapple what he could do, giving the home side the lead. Steele and Walker, with a brace that included his 20th consecutive successful penalty, effectively put the game beyond the reach of the hosts, although they caused a few anxious moments when they grabbed a second.

Then it was back to FA Cup action at a building site formerly known as Kingfield and the fourth leg of the continuing saga of Woking versus Barnet. The game went to extra-time, Barnet missed a penalty in front of the skeleton of the new stand and goals from Hay and Steele ended The Bees' cup hopes for another season, Woking winning 2-1 in front of 3,535 fans.

The evergreen Walker had never really come out in print about how he had come to be playing for The Cards and he wrote an article for the club, giving an insight into just what lured him to Kingfield. Much of the credit must go to Colin Lippiatt as it was he, the number two in the management team, who had contacted the player after he had appeared in a pre-season friendly for Slough Town. Thank goodness Walker, as he revealed in his notes, had the presence of mind to contact Lippiatt after not hearing from Woking for a few days. The fact that he could have been playing elsewhere hardly bears thinking about.

Kidderminster managed to put the skids under Woking's winning run in the Conference by gaining a 0-0 draw at Kingfield, but things could have been worse. Dave Timothy paid the price for hauling down Lee Hughes – who later went on to bigger and better things with West Brom and Coventry – when he was clean through on goal. Timothy was shown the red card but Kiddie were unable to capitalise on either the free-kick, or playing against ten men.

Enfield always presented a tough challenge and a visit to north London in the FA Cup second round was next on the agenda. The ICIS Premier League outfit were managed by George Borg and teams under his leadership certainly lacked nothing in terms of spirit, while they often had a lot of flair and skill to offer as well. Hoddle had been released by Chapple a couple of months earlier and the midfielder found himself on the bench at Southbury Road for the home side. In first-half stoppage time Justin Gentle broke the deadlock and it took a Walker wonder goal to earn a replay. By that time Enfield had been reduced to ten men after Jimmy Carstairs kicked John Crumplin. There was no chance of the replay being held at Kingfield because of the continued building work and – after a 3-2 win away to Runcorn in the league – it was a case of heading off to Adams Park, home of Wycombe Wanderers, to fight for the right to take on Swindon Town in the next round. Hay, who was subjected to some appalling racist chants, rammed the words back down the throats of his detractors by grabbing both Woking goals in a richly deserved 2-1 win. A trip to The County Ground in Wiltshire was confirmed.

Given Woking's record in the competition, it almost goes without saying that the Bob Lord Trophy match away to Slough Town resulted in a 3-0 defeat. Dagenham &

The prolific Darran Hay receiving the plaudits from his adoring public.

Redbridge, firmly rooted to the bottom of the Conference, were the visitors on Boxing Day. Fortunately they settled for a 2-2 draw rather than a repeat of the Christmas stuffing they delivered a year earlier, but nevertheless two valuable points dropped at home was not good. Chapple had often been criticised for his policy on substitutions and his Christmas notes went some way to explaining his position:

My philosophy is that the players' job is for 90 minutes and if those on the pitch are performing as well as they can then I will not normally change things... In each game I pick what I believe to be our best line-up. If one player is clearly not performing then a substitution may be appropriate. Another thing to remember is that with a limited number of players available it is not always possible to have suitable replacements for all areas of the pitch.

He then fantasised over the prospect of beating Swindon in the FA Cup – in a replay if necessary – and then being drawn away to Manchester United. The chance would come after two more league points were wasted with a 0-0 draw to Dagenham in east London.

The FA Cup folklore that surrounded Woking was built on exciting football, gaining results against the odds and heroic displays. Sadly, those ingredients failed to board the team coach for the journey down the M4 and in what was a strangely subdued performance all hope of even a replay had evaporated long before the final whistle signalled a comprehensive 2-0 win for the home club.

It must have prompted Chapple to add to his attacking options because for the next encounter, a Conference clash at Morecambe, there was another striker among the

Super Scotty Steele performs from his bag of tricks at Barnet.

ranks. Chapple could never resist signing players, despite his claims that there was little in the way of finance to allow him to do so. But this particular choice was a surprise to everybody at the club. Nobody had heard of Junior Hunter before the match on the Lancashire coast. However, soon after 4.45 p.m. that Saturday afternoon his name was on everybody's lips – including the stunned home contingent. In a sensational debut, Hunter hit four goals and displayed stunning pace that simply tore the Morecambe defence to shreds. It helped his new team-mates to a one-goal victory, but, given that Woking managed to concede four themselves, it is just as well he had been signed. The 1,312 people who watched the incredible events unfold were certainly enthralled and the late Eric Morecambe, whose statue stands on Morecambe sea front, would have approved of the entertainment level just down the road. While that match will always be remembered for Hunter's debut, it also marked the first goal for Thompson.

Epsom and Ewell were then crushed 6-0 in the Surrey Senior Cup and there was a justifiable confidence about the trip to Carshalton as The Cards set out to retain the FA Trophy for an unprecedented third year. Carshalton manager Fred Callaghan knew a thing or two about Chapple, having been his number two at Kingfield during the famous FA Cup exploits in 1991. On entering the ground it was more akin to paying a visit to the local DIY centre – what appeared to be sharp sand was liberally spread all over the pitch. To say that the tactic affected Woking is a gross understatement and in controversial circumstances the bitter taste of defeat lingered. What was needed on the day was discipline and that was sadly lacking, with Lloyd Wye and Walker both being sent off. Much ado was made of the 3-1 defeat but all suggestions of a protest fell on deaf FA ears. Chapple, as usual, was diplomatic when commenting on the day, saying:

On arriving at the ground Carshalton officials apologised to me about the state of the pitch. I have to say that having seen it earlier in the week, I was surprised that it needed that amount of sand on it. Sharp sand with stones and pebbles in it will not be conducive to any flowing football.

Having suffered disappointment at having to relinquish the trophy they had so proudly defended the previous season, the next fixture was also all about silverware. Molesey visited Kingfield in the Surrey Senior Cup and Hunter again demonstrated his lethal combination of pace and the ability to put the ball in the net. With Woking winning 8-1, the hero of the Morecambe game took his tally to seven goals from three games and he had achieved cult status in just ten days. Surely Hunter had created a club record by scoring hat-tricks on both his home and away debuts? Unfortunately, he was missing when Bromsgrove Rovers played in front of the newly opened Leslie Gosden Stand. Woking could not afford to drop points, with Stevenage Borough and Macclesfield Town starting to pull away from the pack. However, it was another case of opportunities wasted and points dropped in a 1-1 draw which marked the Woking debut of Paul Wanless, signed on loan from Lincoln City. Nevertheless, the atmosphere was tremendous and the excitement generated by those sampling the relative luxury of sitting in the new 2,000 seat structure stayed for a good few months.

John Crumplin gets in a trademark cross at Enfield.

Crystal Palace were the semi-final opponents in the Surrey Senior Cup and a 0-0 draw was the last thing Chapple needed. He wanted as free a fixture list as possible with several players out through injury. However, come the Saturday, come the man. Hunter was back for the visit of Telford United. The visitors kicked off – and after less than 30 seconds Hunter had ensured they would be kicking-off again rather sooner than they could have imagined. Lightning pace had seen him put The Cards ahead before the Telford substitutes had even reached the dugout. In what was his second home match, the in-form predator notched yet another hat-trick in a resounding 5-1 win and in the process the club picked up its 250th point in the top flight of the non-League game.

More goals were to come during the following week, although Woking failed to record a win on both occasions. Hunter grabbed a brace at Dover and Hay came off the bench to grab a goal at The Crabble, but Dover Athletic ran out 4-3 winners and once again found that it suited them to play against The Cards.

Southport were cruising to a home win when they led 2-0 at half-time but Walker and yes, that man Hunter again, salvaged a point in a 2-2 draw. By this time Stevenage, the side Chapple thought were good enough to win the Conference, were leading the table on goal difference from Macclesfield and were five points ahead of Woking. The gap widened further when two more points were tossed away following a 1-1 draw at home to Kettering Town, although Hunter managed to score against one of his former clubs and duly signed a two-and-a-half year contract.

With Wanless having finished his loan spell, Chapple sprung a huge surprise with his team selection for the visit of Welling United. The visitors included ex-Cards Gwynne Berry, Dereck Brown and Ollie Morah, but Chapple had re-signed a man whose

Running out at Swindon in the FA Cup third round.

presence had been an essential part in achieving Conference status. Trevor Baron came into the side in place of Wanless, several seasons after his last Woking appearance.

Returning heroes are always assured of a warm welcome at Kingfield and the graceful Baron certainly received one before a 3-2 Cards triumph. After a run of four goals in three games Hunter failed to get on the scoresheet and many were wondering whether he had lost the knack of putting the ball in the net – or whether the club were fed up with presenting him with the matchball. John Crumplin, Steele and Hay obliged with the goals on this occasion, the first being the 250th scored in the Conference history of the club. Hunter also drew blanks in the next two games, a 2-0 defeat away to Altrincham and a 2-0 win at Farnborough. The Cards booked their place in the Surrey Senior Cup final with a 4-1 win over Crystal Palace in the semi-final replay but by this time they trailed Stevenage by a massive 13 points in the league, albeit with a game in hand on their Hertfordshire rivals. It was payback time when Dover Athletic made a rare Saturday visit to Kingfield and a 3-0 win made up some of the lost ground.

Stuart Girdler was something of a rarity at Woking. He was young and had worked his way from the youth team and reserves into the first-team squad. His moment of glory came in a midweek match at Telford when he scored in a 2-1 win. To say that his celebration was exuberant hardly pays it credit and he subsequently admitted that the older heads told him to calm down as he risked running out of energy.

Walker, with the first of his two goals being the 50th he had scored in Conference football, helped ensure that Hednesford Town were soundly beaten and suddenly the gap at the top of the Conference was down to manageable proportions. The game also

'Laurence is our leader' – Batty up in arms at The County Ground.

marked the 50th clean sheet that Laurence Batty had kept at the top level. Stevenage now had just a 4-point advantage with a game in hand and nine fixtures outstanding.

Woking had a massive Easter programme, with a home game against Macclesfield Town on the Saturday followed by the 'title decider' at Broadhall Way on Easter Monday. The Macclesfield match drew more than 4,500 spectators to Kingfield and is still remembered as one of the great occasions and one of many people's favourite memories. Hunter put Woking ahead with a stunning goal before being sent off following a second caution. His first offence had been to kick an opponent in the backside as he had had the audacity to obstruct Hunter. It was a funny moment but threatened to cost Woking points. Macclesfield took advantage and went 2-1 ahead before half-time. As if that was not bad enough Girdler suffered a sickening knee injury while preventing a certain goal, a moment that would keep him out of the game for many months. Chapple threw substitute Darren Adams into the fray and he delivered what was required in some style. His brace ripped the heart out of the visitors and the atmosphere around the ground surely tested the nuts and bolts holding the roof of the new stand. With ten men and against the odds, The Cards held on for what seemed like 25 hours let alone minutes and the final whistle was accompanied by an emotional outburst from the home support. This 3-2 victory had been something special.

With hardly any time to draw breath it was time to face Stevenage in their backyard. Chapple took the decision to drop Hunter to the bench, bringing Hay back into the attack after he had missed the Macclesfield encounter. Woking had a proud record in Hertfordshire, but that counted for nothing once the action got underway. The home

Andy Ellis on the mark against Bromsgrove Rovers.

Dave Timothy – Speedster who was a popular player with the fans at Kingfield.

side controlled proceedings from start to finish in a 4-0 win as The Cards froze on a day that called for them to be at their resilient best. Perhaps the effort against Macclesfield 48 hours earlier had taken too much out of the players. Whatever the cause, the result meant just one thing – the title was not destined for Surrey. Chapple was generous in defeat and paid tribute to the winners. He also, quite rightly, pointed out that Woking were on course to become the first team ever to have three consecutive top-three Conference finishes. That didn't make up for the disappointment of losing out to a side that were not eligible to be promoted to the Football League, but it did highlight a level of achievement that was not to be sneezed at.

Hay ensured a 1-0 home win over Gateshead, in what was Batty's 150th Conference appearance, and it was still mathematically possible to overhaul Stevenage. That remained the case after a tense 2-1 home win against Farnborough Town. However, things were as good as finished when The Cards could only manage a 2-2 draw away to lowly Halifax Town. Credit is due to the players for fighting back from 2-0 down, despite an enthusiastic public address operator who insisted on giving updates on how Stevenage were getting on.

Away from the trials of the Conference, the club had a cup final to contest. The Surrey Senior Cup was staged at Kingsmeadow, home of Kingstonian, and Tooting & Mitcham United were the opposition. Walker, with a brace, settled what was something of an ill-tempered affair, but the highlight for some revolved around antics off the playing area. Chapple, having espied a Tooting fan who was about to launch a corner flag into the crowd, promptly tackled the miscreant and sat on him until the police arrived. No lasting damage was done and yet again all could see just how much in love with all aspects of the game the genial Woking manager was. He undoubtedly prevented an unpleasant situation from getting out of hand and in the process added another paragraph to the folklore that surrounded him.

Although the realists conceded that Stevenage would be crowned champions, it was Woking's 3-0 defeat away to Northwich Victoria that finally confirmed the fact. Northwich were at Kingfield some three days later and a significantly lower attendance than had been the norm throughout the season looked on as two more points slipped away in a 0-0 draw.

The season ended with a convincing 4-0 home win against Southport, leaving everyone to think of what might have been. Chapple looked back on the season in the Southport programme and made the point that the first five away matches had been tough but that no side had managed to complete the double over his charges. All in all he shielded his disappointment well. There was no shame in finishing in the runner-up spot for the second successive season. There was still a bad taste in the mouth after the farce of the Carshalton FA Trophy exit but there was every reason to believe that the club could return better and stronger the next year.

On top of the achievements on the pitch there was a stand that had no equal in Conference football. Surely the pieces of the jigsaw were falling into place and the club was on the verge of cementing its position at the top of the non-League tree and making that quantum leap forward to the Football League. If only everything in life was that simple.

5

Chapple – Going? Going? Gone
1996/97

From the start this was a strange and unsettling season – albeit one of the most successful in the club's history in terms of glory both in the FA Cup and FA Trophy. Despite the bandwagon continuing to roll on the pitch there were clear divisions between some of the players, while the seemingly non-stop reports of manager Geoff Chapple possibly leaving if he could not gain a contract simply added to the feelings of disquiet and concern.

In his notes for the pre-season games Chapple said: "The season is no sooner over than I am allegedly on the trail of this player and that player. I will not be pressurised into signing anyone who I feel is not right for Woking Football Club." They were clear words from the manager who subsequently announced himself pleased with a 19-man squad that included new faces Terry Howard and Simon Garner from Wycombe Wanderers, Steve Wood from Oxford United, Robin Taylor from Dagenham & Redbridge and Tom Jones from Reading.

Many fans were surprised at the recruitment of the veteran Garner, despite his record of scoring goals for fun in the full-time game. However, Chapple was adamant he was the man to put the ball in the net and that he would be a vital cog in a push for promotion. However, having got on the wrong side of the law, Garner's enforced spell behind bars prevented him from putting the ball under any on a football pitch. In any case, he had already gone out on loan to Walton & Hersham. So much for his help in achieving promotion. His contract was cancelled.

On the pitch the season started perfectly. On a beautifully warm afternoon in Morecambe, the side managed to secure its first ever opening-day victory in the Conference. Darran Hay and Junior Hunter were the scorers who rewrote the history books.

There was drama on the following Tuesday evening when it took late goals from Steve Thompson and Taylor to salvage a point against a visiting Bath City side reduced to ten men. Delight at gaining a point was one thing, but the reality was that Bath were not a good side and the writing on the wall was in large, bold letters. The more optimistic dismissed it as being a symptom of every visiting side wanting to bring Woking's long unbeaten home run to an end.

Hednesford Town suffered the backlash of the display against Bath and only a magnificent display by Scott Cooksey in The Pitmen's goal kept the scale of their defeat down to a decent margin of just 2-0. Andy Ellis 'enjoyed' his five minutes of fame when he became the first player to be booked by a woman referee at senior level, Wendy

Steve Foster and friends in the net against Millwall.

Toms doing the honours. Toms was making her debut as a Conference referee in the home game against Telford United and a lot of fuss was made about the occasion. Match officials do have a part to play but it was overkill from start to finish. Nevertheless, the effervescent Chapple could not resist making comment on the appointment of Toms, saying: "My only concern for her today is our one and only Derek Powell (fixture secretary). I always said that Derek would marry a referee, so be on your guard Wendy."

Next up in the Conference was Dover. For whatever reason, Woking never seemed to excel at The Crabble but an early goal from Thompson gave the fans some hope. However, David Leworthy, who always seemed to relish playing Woking, made the most of the occasion and helped himself to a hat-trick as the Channel port side stormed to a 5-1 win in a match that ended with Wood sustaining a fractured bone in his foot.

Some pride was restored when goals from Clive Walker and Hay were enough to take the points in an away win against Stalybridge Celtic, but within days 'Fortress Kingfield' was stormed for the first time in around two years, and, of all clubs, it was Farnborough Town that achieved the milestone. Ironically, their deserved win came on a night when Colin Fielder, who had served both clubs magnificently, had what was probably his least effective game in a Woking shirt.

Desperate times call for desperate measures and ahead of the game at Altrincham Chapple took the bold step of dropping Walker to the bench. However, only minutes into the game Lloyd Wye was caught out and the home side took the lead. Predictably,

Clive Walker and Robin Taylor – goalscorers at Cambridge United.

the turning point came when Walker, who had had a quiet start to the season, came off the bench. Almost immediately he delivered a trademark quality cross that defender Mark Maddox headed, with some style it has to be said, into his own net to make it 1-1.

Rushden & Diamonds had never scored first in a Conference game but that all changed when they took the lead at Kingfield. However, a Walker hat-trick, which included two penalties, and a goal from Jones – on the green, green grass of home – did the trick. Dover were unable to repeat their home performance, Woking managing to restrict them to a point in a 1-1 draw at Kingfield.

Four days later, with no Conference fixture on the Saturday, the club took on the Kuwait national side. Very few spectators thought the game worth bothering about but it was a tremendous piece of public relations work with widespread media coverage.

It was after a match away to Slough Town that Chapple came out with a confusing quote. Soundly and deservedly beaten 3-0, he went on record as saying that it was "our best display of the season to date". This was not something that too many could identify with from behind the perimeter fence but managers do tend to see things that others don't and there is always more to a contest than just the final score.

Another defeat was just around the corner and it was Macclesfield Town who inflicted it. With John Gregory standing in for Laurence Batty, the game proved to be the final appearance for Fielder who, after being an unused substitute for the following couple of games, left to join Yeovil Town. Fielder had been an inspirational signing for the club and his partnership with Kevan Brown was something that proved awesome time after time. It was a sad day when Fielder departed. His achievements were enormous and thousands had shared his joy when he scored the goal that won the

Junior Hunter up to his own brand of tricks at Coventry City.

1995 FA Trophy Final. He provided all Woking fans with a treat in watching a real craftsman at work during his four or so years at the club.

With arch rivals Stevenage Borough making a midweek trip to Kingfield, Chapple had the courage to make wholesale changes and he was rewarded with a great display from the side. In came Steve Foster for the bargain price of £9,000, Grant Payne was back again and Giuliano Grazioli was signed on loan from Peterborough United. Shane Wye returned to the ranks and summer signing Howard was fit at long last.

Stevenage were swept aside and the confidence gained from that game travelled all the way up to Halifax a few days later. Grazioli grabbed a hat-trick and Walker recorded another success from the penalty spot. It was all too much for the home team as they succumbed 4-0 and had two players sent off in the process. The momentum continued back at Kingfield. Although Richard Nugent, who never really captured the imagination of the Woking fans, scored for Kettering, the Grazioli and Walker combination sent the Northamptonshire outfit back home pointless.

The clamour to sign Grazioli was growing by the day and it was hard to know what to make of it all. Potential transfer fee costs were seemingly plucked out of the air and the whole saga became something of a joke when viewed from the outside. Clearly Chapple wanted the player, clearly the crowd wanted him and from what everybody was told, the player wanted to join. The sticking point, reportedly, was that the directors would not sanction the amount asked for by Peterborough. Chapple made his views clear when he said: "The final decision rests with the management committee and I am entirely in their hands over the matter." Fortunately, Grazioli was still around long enough to put the skids under Stevenage once again, scoring after just 15 seconds at Broadhall Way and then adding a second as Woking strolled to an emphatic 3-0 win.

After a comfortable victory against Northwich Victoria, it was time for an enthralling FA Cup tie against Division Two leaders Millwall. Foster had backed himself to score the first goal of the game and he was right to trust his own judgement. On a rock-hard pitch that had a covering of frost, Walker showed incredible ball control and skill to beat Northern Ireland international Anton Rogan on the touchline and deliver an inch perfect cross for Foster to rise at the far post and bravely head into the back of the net. Millwall showed their pedigree by fighting back to take the lead but after Hunter was upended Walker made it 2-2 from the spot.

Scott Steele salvaged a point at Bath with a late goal, but the impression was that the players had their minds on the Millwall replay. In the rematch the team showed tremendous resilience as The Lions threw everything at the Woking rearguard. Walker scored the only goal – a superb strike in the ninth minute after he latched onto a magnificent pass from Jones. Each and every player excelled and even the Millwall fans joined in the applause at the final whistle, despite seeing their side lose at home for only the second time since the start of the season. Some of their more notorious followers were not quite so impressed, however, and despite a police escort several of the Woking coaches sustained damage following roadside ambushes.

Cards' fans enjoying their day out at Highfield Road.

Thommo at Kingfield – the man who booked the replay with The Sky Blues.

The euphoria of winning at The New Den was deflated by constant stories that Walker was about to join Rushden & Diamonds. There were more plots and counter-plots than any self-respecting Australian soap opera could conjure up. Where were the voices of reason in all of this? After all, Walker was a contracted Woking player and somebody should have come out with a resolute statement to that effect. However, that never happened and it didn't take a genius to realise that the harmony portrayed was little more than a sham.

Despite the obvious rift amongst some players they gelled well enough to thrash Altrincham 7-1, but the crowd still yearned for Grazioli – who, by pure coincidence, was back at Woking, in the stand – as they roared to their best ever win in the Conference. The Grazioli saga continued, reaching farcical proportions, with comments in the press by the manager and club officials. Quite why the whole sorry episode had to be acted out in public only those who took part can say. Despite all of this, a return of seven points out of nine saw the team rise to third place in the table by the end of November. But the onset of winter saw the team return to Jekyll and Hyde performances.

A thorough beating at home by Welling United, thanks to goals from former Cards Lennie Dennis and Barry Lakin, added to the appalling record of just one win in five seasons of Bob Lord Trophy football (in its many guises). Not to worry as there were bigger fish to fry.

Victory over Millwall had been rewarded with an FA Cup second-round tie at Cambridge United. Walker and Taylor both scored as the home side – top of Division Three at the time – went out of the competition 2-0. Walker's goal was top class and it seemed extremely petulant of Roy McFarland, the former England international who was managing Cambridge, to describe the chip shot from the touchline as a fluke.

Even after that great result there was no let up in the speculation over Walker's future. When prompted by a BBC radio reporter, the player said that he didn't know which club he would be with by the time the draw for the third round was made. It seemed that no matter what happened on the pitch everybody wanted to have their say off it.

But the team was having difficulty in getting their say on the pitch too. The Surrey Senior Cup became a distant memory after Woking crashed out in humiliating style to Walton & Hersham. It was painful to watch but not so for Chapple. He was at Highfield Road watching The Cards' next FA Cup opponents Coventry City. The Premiership club were having a lean time of things, but Chapple watched them beat high-flying Newcastle United – just the result nobody connected with Woking wanted as the tie loomed large.

Woking looked to put themselves back on track again as Halifax Town, who were destined to regain their Football League status, were swept aside during a storming opening 45 minutes. But 2-0 is widely regarded as the hardest lead to maintain and with Woking unsure whether to go for the third or defend in numbers, the Yorkshiremen duly took a point, coming back to 2-2.

Boxing Day saw the return of Hunter, the forgotten striking hero of Kingfield, to the side that played at Hayes. He obliged with two goals but the home team, who were struggling for Conference survival, were grateful as Woking snatched defeat from the jaws of victory by conceding two late goals to lose 3-2. Slough Town, also struggling, failed to make any impression on a 2-0 Woking lead but they were given every opportunity to do so in another below-par performance by Chapple's side.

The New Year started with an FA Trophy tie played on a Sunday afternoon at Wokingham. Steve Thompson's first-half goal settled the outcome but the watching Coventry City scout probably did not give Sky Blues manager Gordon Strachan too much information to cause the Scot any sleepless nights. He would have done well to note the name of the scorer though.

Due to the vagaries of the English weather Woking travelled to their FA Cup third-round match against Coventry three weeks later than the scheduled date – on fourth-round day in fact. The fact that the Premiership side were hardly world-beaters probably didn't dissuade too many people from predicting a comfortable win for them. But Woking held out superbly and Coventry only went ahead after a huge slice of luck. The immensely talented Gary McAllister, bearing only a passing resemblance to a current international on the day, miscued as he attempted to reach a cross. The ball fell kindly for Eoin Jess and Woking were 1-0 down. From that point on Woking dominated the game, and, after great work by Jones and Howard, it was that man Thompson who struck in the 90th minute, leaving keeper Steve Ogrizovic and defender Brian Borrows in the running for the 'most depressed look in football award'. The goal was one of those magic moments.

At the final whistle there was all the excitement of a cup upset and quite rightly so. Woking's players, some of whom were hardly going through their paces in run-of-the-mill games, had done themselves proud. Surely they couldn't be dismissed as 'big time

Scott Steele side-foots Woking level against Coventry City in the FA Cup second round.

Shane Wye, who always gave his all for the
Woking cause.

Charlies'? Chapple made a foray into the transfer market and signed Justin Jackson for
£30,000 from Morecambe. Jackson had made his name with the Lancashire seaside club
but his Woking debut, away to Hednesford Town, was on a day when the side was
distinctly second best once again, losing 2-0.

As the cup replay neared, Coventry hardly endeared themselves to the Woking fans,
making disparaging noises about Woking players being too big for their boots. Once on
the Kingfield turf, Noel Whelan gave Coventry the lead when Batty failed to hold a
McAllister free-kick, although after Steele equalised it was only the heroics of Ogrizovic
that kept Coventry in the match. But the tie was settled when another McAllister free-
kick was deflected into the net off Foster. Batty suggested putting a few bob on the Sky
Blues being relegated. McAllister, meanwhile, questioned how it could be that Woking
were not doing so well in the Conference, suggesting that some players were probably
only putting effort into cup-ties. Neither camp received the comments too well, but
there was more than an element of truth in what both had to say.

Jackson, who had been a spectator for the two cup clashes, scored in the FA Trophy
tie away to St Albans City, but it took a replay to see off the Hertfordshire side. Chapple,
reflecting how the club had gone out of the competition at Carshalton the previous
season, made it clear that he relished another Wembley appointment.

However, the downward spiral in the Conference continued when Southport, who
had never previously taken so much as a point away from Kingfield, claimed all three
courtesy of a bizarre own goal by Howard. Jackson was on target again in a 3-0 win at
Bromsgrove but the game ended with a nightmare for Woking. Brown conceded a late
penalty. Batty saved the kick but his brave attempt to smother the follow-up attempt
led to him sustaining a broken finger and missing the next five outings.

Penalties featured strongly in the next round of the FA Trophy, a trip to Somerset to
face Dorchester Town. Premiership referee Mike Reed was very much in the news after a
controversial penalty award cost Leicester City dearly in a FA Cup clash at Chelsea.

Andy Ellis nets the vital goal at Heybridge Swifts in the FA Trophy quarter-final.

Chapple had brought in Hans Segers in goal for the injured Batty. The former Wimbledon keeper was on trial at the time following match-rigging allegations. That Reed and Segers should come face to face in the FA Trophy was not high on the list of probabilities.

Woking twice had to come from behind in order to make progress. Reed, from a distance, adjudged that Segers had conceded a penalty. The Dutchman pulled off a great save but was let down by his defenders as they stood on in admiration and watched the ball being despatched into the net in the follow-up attempt, giving the home side a 2-1 lead. It was Steele who spared the blushes with a 90th-minute winner that led to a visit to Heybridge Swifts in the wilds of Essex.

In the meantime there were more Conference matches to play. It has to be said that very few of the club's matches ever make the news in all corners of the world. However, across the globe newspapers and radio stations reported that Woking's home match against Hayes had been abandoned due to a problem with the pitch. Many would have dismissed a suggestion that the pitch had collapsed, but that is what happened. As everyone read the next day, Brown 'fell' into a hole that just opened up. Of course there were plenty of laughs about the whole incident and the club received copies of articles published in France, New Zealand and Fiji. But there was a serious side to it all and the upshot of the abandoned game was that fixtures were piling up.

Gateshead was the scene of some of the most appalling antics one could imagine taking place on a football pitch. Quite inexplicably, Jones was sent off after he had been the victim of an elaborate piece of playacting and dreadful refereeing. Things got worse when none of the officials, who had been so quick to pick out Jones, failed to see one of the Gateshead substitutes quite openly kick Shane Wye when he went to collect the

Scott Steele takes on Efetobor Sodge at Broadhall Way in the now legendary FA Trophy semi-final, second leg.

ball for a throw-in. By half-time Woking were 3-0 down and the rationale behind travelling all that way to the north-east surely did not add up for the Woking faithful. Hay and Walker pulled a couple back but to say that the game left a bad taste in the mouth is hardly an adequate sentiment.

Scrappy home wins over Welling United and Stalybridge Celtic paved the way for the Trophy visit to Heybridge. It was not going to be easy. The almost-unheard-of side had dumped Kidderminster Harriers out of the competition with an emphatic 3-0 win and the sight of a hard and uneven pitch did not bode well for a comfortable afternoon. The home team, who were physically very strong, upset any hopes Woking had of playing measured football and it took a scrambled goal from Ellis to settle the game and line up the mouth-watering prospect of a semi-final against Stevenage Borough.

The Conference struggle to get fixtures back on track continued when Hayes arrived at Kingfield. The pitch stayed intact – which is something of a pity as the visitors took all three points to help in their fight against relegation. Telford were beaten, but only just, and by the time Kidderminster arrived Batty was back in goal. With Walker out of the side, a Batty penalty and a goal from Hay did serious damage to Kidderminster's hopes of promotion.

The first leg of the FA Trophy semi-final was played at Kingfield, with Walker still absent through injury. However, just as Grazioli had done at Broadhall Way in the Conference, Taylor got Woking off to a flying start. Jackson did superbly to win the ball and Taylor cut in from the left to blast a rocket of a shot beyond Richard Wilmott with only 31 seconds of the game played. Thompson was lucky to escape serious and permanent injury when he was bundled into the perimeter fence in an incident that went unpunished by Dermot Gallagher, another Premiership referee who failed to impress a non-League audience.

Terry Howard and Lloyd Wye in FA Trophy semi-final action at Stevenage.

From that point it was a case of Woking soaking up pressure and Stevenage wasting chance after chance. Batty was magnificent throughout, pulling off breathtaking saves to deny the potent Stevenage forwards. Taylor's goal was the only one of the match but would it be enough to book a third Wembley appearance in four seasons?

Bromsgrove Rovers arrived at Kingfield in the knowledge that they would be relegated if they lost and Welling United won a few days later. They really need not have worried as they cruised to a 3-1 win, inflicting Woking's heaviest home defeat since Boxing Day 1994 in the process. The performance drew stinging criticism from management and fans alike as it seemed to lack passion as well as any apparent tactics. The tactical naiveté seemed strange. Several of the players had put forward their case for assisting Chapple and assistant Colin Lippiatt and without doubting their credentials, it could be suggested that it was a matter of too many cooks spoiling the broth.

Needless to say, it was a very different attitude in the second leg against Stevenage, ahead of which Chapple had said: "Past experience has shown that they are very good, with their pre-match activities, at getting the crowd going. It will be our job, with your encouragement, to try and silence them."

Despite having Walker back from injury, there was not time to do much silencing when, contrary to what normally happened between the teams, it was Paul Fairclough's side that stormed into an early lead through Barry Hayles following a dreadful piece of defending. With just 41 seconds played the tie was all-square. Brown was sent off but ten men Woking held on to reach extra-time, during which Hay scored. The somewhat fickle home crowd were streaming out of the ground when Gary Crawshaw lobbed Batty – forcing a replay to be held at Watford.

Four days later came the decider. There had been a scare in between when Batty and Ellis had hobbled off during the game at Kidderminster, which had already been marked by several Woking absentees. But Vicarage Road saw goals from Walker and Ellis put Woking firmly in control. It was very much against the run of play when Fairclough's men gained some hope with a late goal by Jason Soloman but it was never going to be enough. Lloyd Wye had been magnificent in the second leg against Stevenage and had been singled out by Chapple for praise. The semi-final replay marked his 500th Woking appearance when he came on as a substitute. However, by the time the season had come to a close Wye had been dropped and made available for transfer.

Behind-the-scenes drama for the game at Watford happened when Thompson very nearly missed the match. His train had broken down and there was every chance he would not make it. Mike Bidmead, at that time the Woking ground and safety officer, drove to Reading to ensure the influential midfielder made it to the stadium in time.

The remaining Conference fixtures were largely academic, but the win away to Northwich Victoria went against Chapple's well publicised views that a team could not win the Conference with youngsters. His hand had been forced by the number of injuries in the squad and a side with a number of 'junior' players in it not only won the game, but also registered Woking's first win at The Drill Field.

Most of the old guard returned for the game at Nene Park against Rushden & Diamonds. If anyone needed proof that the team spirit was poor, then this game drove the point home. Jackson put Woking ahead but not a single Woking player joined in his celebration. Indeed, not long afterwards Jackson and Walker exchanged words in the centre of the pitch. Quite what prompted that piece of drama goodness only knows, but it was unseemly and it took players from both teams to come between the pair of them. Some managers may have reacted by substituting both men – Chapple decided to keep them on the pitch. But such an incident only served to reinforce the belief that things were going badly wrong off the field and that something of serious consequence would unfold at the end of the season.

The final Conference game of the campaign could have left Woking in fourth place, but Morecambe came to Kingfield and looked far more interested in claiming that spot. Chapple didn't witness the 2-1 defeat, as he was reportedly at another game looking at players. Lippiatt was in charge for the day and he earned the respect of a number of supporters by staying around to answer countless questions long after most people had gone home. However, anything he had to say about the following season was sadly irrelevant as he and Chapple were destined to leave in the summer.

All the disappointment of the Conference season, all of the back-stabbing and the moans were cast aside for a few hours at Wembley. Without creating too many chances Woking dominated the game against Dagenham & Redbridge and Hay's extra-time winner sent the Woking contingent among the crowd into raptures. For a short while everybody connected with the club looked happy. The eagle eyes of the press had

Scott Steele relishes the limelight against The Cards' biggest rivals.

Woking – three-time Wembley winners.

noticed something though and the side was reported as being the most miserable looking Wembley winners ever.

Who knows exactly what was going on, but clearly some of the players did not get on too well. There was constant speculation about the futures of Chapple and Lippiatt and much was made about contract talks with newly elected chairman Jon Davies. Plenty of people seemed to have an agenda and each would say they had every right to put their case and protect their best interests.

In his final programme notes of the season Chapple wrote what could now be looked back upon with a certain amount of irony when he said: "We all know that there will be high hopes of the championship next season. After all, we have gone five seasons without winning one, not that we have done too badly in the meantime though."

However, the prospect of the team and the club falling apart produced bad feeling and the fans were becoming restless, despite his fine words, and despite another hugely successful season in the cups which have quite rightly earned their place in folklore. Now a new era was about to begin but nobody could have realised at the time that this was the end of a pretty special one.

6

A New Era
1997/98

Future Woking historians will always refer to the 1990s as the glory years. Up until May 1997, there had been a period of unprecedented success in the FA Cup and the FA Trophy and the club had become a force in the highest echelon of non-League football, pulling in crowds of almost 3,000 on a regular basis. What people did not appreciate at the time was that, as far as Woking Football Club was concerned, this was as good as it was going to get.

If anyone was told at that time that within three years at least a thousand people would be knocked off the average gate and that relegation battles would be the order of the day, they would have laughed out loud. After all, the club had just finished fifth in the Conference, picked up FA Trophy win number three and reached the third round of the FA Cup. Having beaten Division Three leaders Cambridge United and Division Two pacemakers Millwall on their own grounds, The Cards had become the first non-League side to hold a Premiership club, Coventry City, on their own patch. Heady stuff indeed.

But while this record would have satisfied most committees (or boards of directors) at football clubs around the country, it was not considered enough to earn manager Geoff Chapple the security of a contract. The man who had dragged an Isthmian League Division Two South team through the divisions and delivered far more than could ever have been expected in terms of exposure for the town, resigned on 5 June 1997 to become manager of Kingstonian. There are many theories as to why he went. Some say he had been in negotiations with Kingstonian for months and had planned the move. The man himself has always insisted he would have stayed if he had been afforded just a bit of security and that Woking's neighbours from the ICIS Premier Division were offering a four-year deal. Chapple maintains he advised the then chairman Jon Davies of the rival offer and is understood to have been told something along the lines of "that sounds like a good deal." Whatever the rights and wrongs of the story, Chapple departed. He had presided over 742 matches, winning 416, drawing 154 and losing 172.

The overriding goal of the club at that time was to achieve Football League status. There was no doubt the consensus among those who mattered was that Chapple was not the man to take them there. Great cup man, but not someone who could motivate a team over a league season to make that final step. So they said.

There was also something else. The final few months of his reign saw a significant change in dressing room morale. There had been rumblings of discontent among the

New boss John McGovern collects his sponsored car.

players towards the end of the previous season and the general feeling was that there was a lack of unity all round. Had they heard a whisper that their boss was planning to move? Were there too many personalities in the dressing room with something to say? Whatever the reason for the unrest, certain players were airing their dirty washing in public and getting away with it. It was time for Chapple to go and from his point of view what better way than to quit while you are ahead?

Without a contract the pressure would have been on him to make a blistering start to the following season – or become likely to be sacked. At least he had made his decision through his own volition. Whichever way you looked at it, this was the start of where it would, ultimately, all go horribly wrong. The benefit of hindsight is a wonderful luxury and now it is known that the success of the past few years had been taken for granted. With success had come money through the gate and this was a club which did not think for one minute that the fans would stop coming. Around 90 per cent of income was from that source so why worry about commercial activity? Surely that was for businesses, not football clubs? Not so, and the lessons would be learned in time.

John McGovern was a famous name in football. He had a rich and fulfilling career as a player and was a Brian Clough protégé who had lifted the ultimate prize of the European Cup in 1979 and 1980 as Nottingham Forest's captain. Now he was one of around 70 applicants for Chapple's old job. While Clive Walker was undoubtedly the people's choice to take over, Davies and some of his committee had other ideas.

The magnificent Leslie Gosden Stand.

Justin Jackson during his unhappy spell at Kingfield.

McGovern's managerial experience was limited and he hardly set the world alight at Bolton Wanderers, Chorley, Plymouth Argyle and Rotherham. But no matter. The committee wanted a big name and were flattered by McGovern's interest, so much so that he was offered the post 20 days after the hot-seat was vacated. Appointing a manager was not something the club had done for 13 years. The successors to the committee would be far busier in that respect in years to come.

"I hope to maintain and improve upon the style of football that is played here and I want to use my experience to show the players professional methods of doing things," said McGovern upon his arrival. It was unreasonable to expect him to achieve instant results but there was a real expectancy that Woking would follow Macclesfield Town into the Football League. Despite being tempered by the Chapple affair, the optimism that surrounded the club could not have been greater.

With Macclesfield's promotion had come Hereford United's drop to the Vauxhall Conference. The Bulls would prove to be formidable opposition, along with the likes of Halifax Town, Cheltenham Town, Stevenage Borough and Rushden & Diamonds. If The Cards were going to continue to be a force in an ever-strengthening competition they would have to do it without Walker, Steve Foster and the Wye brothers, Shane and Lloyd. By the time Walker was told he was not wanted as a player/boss, the contract offer as a player had been withdrawn. It was clear he was considered surplus to requirements and Woking's loss proved Cheltenham's gain.

Foster was a magnificent defender who enjoyed a superb eight months at the club, having joined from Telford United for £9,000. He was sold for £150,000 – a record

Steve Thompson in typically industrious mood.

which was only to be bettered by the sale of Kevin Betsy for an overall fee of £155,000 the following season. Foster's departure to Bristol Rovers realised a serious profit and could not have done any harm to the club's objective, which was to secure promotion in McGovern's first season.

The Wyes had contributed immeasurably to the success of the club since the mid-1980s, but neither was given a chance to prove themselves under the new boss. Shane headed back to New Zealand, where he had been playing every summer.

Lloyd had previously been told by Chapple that he was no longer part of his plans – and this view was echoed by the new boss. Ironically, and some might say tellingly, the only man who had a higher appearance record than Lloyd was Brian Finn – now McGovern's number two. Left-back Lloyd never played for the club again, while Finn's record remains.

Grant Payne and Scott Smith were added to the squad and the season started unremarkably with 1-1 draws at home to Telford United and away to Welling United. For Payne it was his third spell at the club, having been on loan from Wimbledon in 1995 and 1996. On each of his previous 'debuts' for The Cards he scored and he repeated this trick again against Telford. He made it three in three with one at Park View Road and another in a defeat at Cheltenham.

McGovern's first victory came in the home Bank Holiday clash with Slough Town – managed by a certain Brian McDermott, who Cards' fans would come to know a lot better the following season. Justin Jackson notched his first goal of the campaign in front of a crowd of 2,829. Kevin Betsy, who had made his full Conference debut the previous season at Northwich Victoria and was a real emerging talent, scored his first senior goal against them in a 1-0 win at Kingfield. The Cards were well and truly off and running.

Darran Hay then scored in three consecutive matches which included one win – at Kettering Town – before Steve Thompson converted his first goal of the season in a 2-1 victory at Gateshead. McGovern was still weighing up his squad at that time and had introduced centre half Michael Danzey from Aylesbury United, who linked up with Simon Stewart and Terry Howard in a back three. Kevan Brown had been dropped in favour of Stewart, who was on loan from Fulham, but he was reintroduced once Stewart had returned to Craven Cottage. Danzey was a significant recruit but Jackson paid the price for failing to hit the goalscoring heights he had achieved at his former club, Morecambe. He left Kingfield for Notts County, The Cards reportedly getting their £30,000 back in the transaction.

A 4-0 midweek hammering of Dover Athletic included another landmark in the club's history. Steve West, the club's new record (£35,000) signing from Enfield, was another to score on his debut. But weekends were not so rosy. A 0-0 draw at Stevenage brought about the third consecutive failure to win a Conference match on a Saturday, following a 2-0 home reverse against Morecambe and a 2-1 defeat at Rushden & Diamonds. The previous worst three-weekend sequence had happened in October and November 1992 against Bromsgrove Rovers, Yeovil Town and Gateshead. Still, never before had Woking entered the 10th match of a Conference season (against Morecambe) with the goals against figure still in single figures – a real positive for

Thommo running Morecambe ragged.

McGovern. Previous seasons had seen figures of 16, 18, 12, 13 and 11. This season it had been 9.

McGovern summed up his mixed fortunes, saying:

With a third of the season gone, we are still in touch with the leaders but in my humble opinion, we have definitely not played well as a side. In spells we have been good, but due to the transition of players in and out, the consistency we are striving for has not been apparent. I am confident that the free-flowing football we are capable of will soon be there for all to appreciate.

While Junior Hunter was another to leave the club, centre half Richard Goddard was signed for £7,000 from Brentford and Wayne Sutton, hardly the most mobile midfielder ever to wear a Woking shirt, joined from Derby County. Many Woking fans thought that the following weeks revealed why Derby boss Jim Smith was, according to McGovern, "more than helpful in clearing any obstacles that may have scuppered the move". Smith, they said, always was a shrewd judge of a player. McGovern had used either Tom Jones or Andy Ellis at various times alongside Thompson in midfield. Now he preferred the rotund Sutton, not one ever destined to grace the club's Hall of Fame. And that was being kind.

Following a 3-1 win against Stalybridge Celtic, Woking were fourth in the Conference with 30 points from 17 matches (including just 3 defeats) and were sat behind a trio of Towns – Hednesford, Halifax and Cheltenham. Then came the first round of the FA Cup and a match which saw a turning point. Football League Division Two strugglers

Junior Hunter – anything could happen and it often did.

Southend United arrived at Kingfield having hardly won an away match in 12 months. They had just lost their seventh away fixture out of eight since the start of the season, a 5-1 collapse at Grimsby Town who themselves had scored only four times in their seven previous home matches. Even the *Southend Evening Echo* had been quoted as saying: "Woking's home record gives Southend hope as they have drawn two and lost one of their seven Conference home games". United boss Alvin Martin had to counter pessimism, adding: "We certainly won't go to Woking like lambs to the slaughter. We're the league side."

From 1991 up until that point, Woking had been on the crest of a wave in the competition and had a reputation which obviously worried the life out of their opponents. But, with little awareness of Woking's tradition, McGovern seemed not understand why Woking had been made favourites in the circumstances and insisted in the programme notes: "We have been tipped in many quarters to win today's match. The reality is, if we wish to get anything from Southend, we have to match their professionalism and compete as if our lives depended on it." His negative approach was reflected in a performance which saw The Cards rarely venture over the halfway line in a 2-0 defeat totally out of character. McGovern had expected to lose and said afterwards: "Frankly I was overwhelmed and indeed baffled by the one-sided publicity in our favour which preceded the game. I was totally bemused that we were made favourites against Southend United of the Football League Division Two."

The Essex club celebrated their win as though they were the giant killers, another aspect that puzzled McGovern. The whole episode summed up his knowledge of Woking Football Club and the league they were playing in. His lack of empathy and respect for those who were playing for him shone through at that time like a beacon.

His programme notes often referred to goings on in the Premiership and it was clear to many Cards' fans that he felt he belonged somewhere else.

Nevertheless, 3,319 people turned up at Kingfield for the next home match, a 2-2 draw with Halifax Town. Three successive 3-0 wins in the Conference followed, the last in front of the season's best crowd, 4,124, against Farnborough Town. Danzey and Payne scored in all three. Beating Yeovil Town 2-0 was followed by a three-goal defeat in the return match against Farnborough at Cherrywood Road in atrocious conditions. Sandwiched in between was a Surrey Senior Cup tie against Croydon Athletic, in which Scott Steele scored an incredible goal by chipping the keeper from 45 yards. It was a shame only 426 turned out to see it.

On the playing side Eddie Saunders had joined from Carshalton Athletic and Howard was soon to leave the club for Yeovil Town. Another cup defeat, this time to Southern League side Margate, was another disappointing affair and was largely down to poor finishing. McGovern had been confident of a success, as his programme notes read:

Today marks the start of a month in which we will play only one league match. With a Spalding Cup tie against Farnborough, a Surrey Senior Cup match and a second FA Trophy round on the 31st, our only Conference encounter is against Stalybridge.

Thanks to the Margate defeat, it was a case of make that no game on the 31st.

During February, Betsy had been under the watchful eye of Kevin Keegan at Fulham and had impressed the future England boss. History would show it was the beginning of an exciting development in the life of the young star. Saturday 7 March became a

Rising star Kevin Betsy has a go against Stalybridge Celtic.

'Steady' Eddie Saunders takes to the sky against Kettering Town.

significant date when Brown played his last match for The Cards – for the time being at least. Despite being in the form of his life, he was sold to Yeovil Town three games after making his 300th competitive appearance for The Cards, while Goddard assumed his role at the heart of Woking's defence. Grown men cried as Brown bade his farewell, although McGovern is understood to have declared himself happy in a public meeting to have got £7,500 for a "35-year-old". Unfortunately for him the player's father stood up in the same room and retorted, "Actually he's 31". Brown had been the only player to have played alongside everyone else at Woking at Conference level.

Another fantastic servant for Woking was discarded in the same week. Steve Thompson made his 120th and final appearance for the club (with only one as a substitute), in the Surrey Senior Cup semi-final win over Chertsey Town five days before Brown departed. Rod McAree, who arrived on loan from Fulham, was his replacement but history will reveal that it was 'Thommo' who made by far the bigger impact at Kingfield before he too went to join Colin Lippiatt at Yeovil Town, this time for £5,000.

Andy Ellis took over from Brown as skipper and when he led the team out on a Tuesday night at Slough it coincided with his 150th full appearance. Not only did Woking win 3-1, they became the first visiting side to score in the Conference at Wexham Park since Cheltenham Town a little more than four months before.

By the time Rushden & Diamonds arrived in Surrey for a massive clash the two teams were locked on 59 points, with Woking in second place courtesy of their superior goal difference, although still nine points adrift of eventual champions Halifax Town.

The 2-0 defeat, in which Laurence Batty became only the seventh player in the club's history to make 350 appearances, was a crushing blow to any ambitions The Cards had of keeping pace with the league leaders and McGovern commented: "Our dressing room after that defeat was like a morgue, with faces drawn and heads bowed. As a side we had not played well enough to win and were disconsolate to a man."

West took the brunt of the criticism after the match in a similar way to that of Hay against Margate. Missed chances had cost the team dear at a crucial time, although in truth Woking were outplayed. But still, The Cards had conceded just 29 goals in their opening 31 league matches, while in each of the five previous seasons they had leaked more than 40 by that stage. The 55 goals scored in that time had been exceeded just twice before and the goal difference was superior. With Hay due to miss four matches through suspension, McGovern drafted in Andy Hayward on loan from his old club Rotherham United to add firepower to his attack.

The Rushden result had a huge bearing on the subsequent home attendance, which dropped from 3,930 to 2,384 for the visit of Kidderminster Harriers – who, despite being one of the better footballing teams in the division, were not having the best of seasons. Another defeat put an end to any lingering title hopes for Woking but they at least put on a super show. Betsy and Hayward had a field day down both flanks and the only surprise was that the ball never found its way into the Harriers net. "We must have had 90 per cent of possession in the first half, created lots of openings, but amazingly we never managed to finish one of them," mused McGovern. "In the first half I have

Grant Payne and Robin Taylor celebrate against Welling United.

never seen us play better. With a bit more luck or good fortune we could have gone in at half-time three or four goals up."

But Woking lost and on a day when Telford United beat fourth-place Cheltenham, and Halifax overcame the challenge of Rushden, the title race was all but over. "After Saturday, Halifax have cleaned out everybody," said McGovern. "Had they lost and we won then you would have thought we were still close enough. It would take a massive turn of events now to stop them winning the title."

The Cards still had two cup finals to look forward to, despite the fact their league ambitions had all but disappeared. A double-legged Spalding Cup final – the Conference league cup – against Morecambe and a clash with Kingstonian in the Surrey Senior beckoned. Neither whetted the appetite to any great degree but as the only items on the menu it was a case of being grateful for small mercies. Just 782 turned out to watch the first meeting against Morecambe on the Lancashire Coast, a 1-1 draw thanks to Hayward's first goal for The Cards just five minutes into the contest.

A third successive Conference defeat at the hands of Hereford United at Edgar Street followed, prompting McGovern to say:

I'm very sad because we've lost a football match. As a manager I've got to try and put a team together that wins matches and we didn't today. But I can't complain about the effort of the players because that has been tremendous.

By the time Stevenage Borough – who like Kidderminster Harriers had endured a difficult season in the bottom half of the Conference – arrived in Surrey for everybody's favourite meeting, Woking were seven points behind Rushden and an incredible 17 behind runaway leaders Halifax. They were now looking over their shoulders at the likes of Morecambe, Hereford, Hednesford and Cheltenham who were chasing third place.

Paul Fairclough's Boro presented a tough challenge nonetheless and McGovern was keen to get another win under his belt as reward for his team's hard work.

A cracker of a match was as entertaining as any previously seen at Kingfield during the season, with The Cards scoring four times in the final 15 minutes to turn a 2-1 deficit into a 5-3 victory. Hayward bagged an impressive double, while McAree, Payne and West were also on target. Payne became the first player during the campaign to come off the bench and score in a league game. West had done the same with a couple against Leatherhead but that was in the Surrey Senior Cup. "We've played twice as well as that in the last three games and lost so that sums up what a crazy night it was," remarked McGovern. "Anybody looking for defences to defend and a side that was well-balanced, did not get that tonight but what they got was an exciting game of football."

His thoughts on the forthcoming visit to the champions elect were straightforward. "If we play like that against Halifax we'll lose 10-0." In fact it was only 1-0 against a side who all but wrapped up the title as Rushden lost to Telford on the same day.

Four more wins for The Cards were accompanied by defeats at Leek Town and Hayes, the latter by 3-0. There was to be no silverware adorning the trophy cabinet by the season's end. A 1-1 draw with Morecambe in the Spalding Cup final second leg at Kingfield ended in a penalty shoot out which went in favour of the visitors, while Kingstonian lifted the Surrey Senior Cup after a replay.

So, McGovern's Woking finished third in the final reckoning after a season in which he had made as many enemies as he had friends. Setting Betsy on the road to a Football League career – he was named by rival managers in the Conference team of the year – by giving him a regular place, was the major plus. Getting rid of Brown in his prime was an unforgivable mistake in many people's eyes.

As the fans reflected on a season in which much happened on the playing side, the club finally shrugged off its members club tag as it became a limited company. Davies was re-elected chairman of the new board with John Taylor, Bill Sutton, Phil Ledger, Michael Church, Graham Elmer and Paul Elmer voted in as directors. There was no place on the board for Terry Molloy, a man who was unhappy at being overlooked in the new regime, although he was destined to be chairman in the future. For now, he was diplomatic outwardly, although privately seething at his omission. "I am very, very disappointed because in the past six years I have given all I have to the club," he said. "I have done every job and any job and I was hoping that would continue into the new era. I have been one of the two negotiators involved with the solicitors on incorporation over the past two years and in that sense I am disappointed." Actually, in football speak, he was gutted. After being a major player in the work behind the scenes, he quite rightly felt angry, although he vowed to continue as a "keen and eager supporter".

Kevin Betsy enjoys possession against Rushden & Diamonds.

Steve West scoring v. Hereford United, as Grant Payne jumps for joy.

Davies announced: "It is a very big step in the history of Woking Football Club. It is now a limited company and the incorporation was needed to progress into the Football League." Everybody seemed to be getting carried away with the fact that Woking would go up at some stage – no question. They forgot to appreciate that finishing top of the division was what was needed to fulfil their aim and despite having a former European Cup-winning captain in charge it was to remain a pipe dream.

Meanwhile, following Woking Borough Council and Fox Garage's decisions to reduce their involvement on the sponsorship side, The Cards made another big announcement – a new shirt sponsor had come on board. Byfleet company MX, a telephone control centre for both property and computer maintenance, were happy to lend their name to Woking as shirt sponsors. The only problem as far as the club was concerned was that the contract was allegedly never signed. The deal was to eventually turn sour, with The Cards claiming money owed and with the company able to side-step payment on the grounds that the deal was not legally bound. It was a serious error and was indicative of the fortunes about to befall the club. It was also an example of the lack of business nous at Kingfield and in time the lack of funds from commercial activities would begin to bite harder than anyone involved could ever have imagined.

But the question back then was still, would McGovern be able to build on the season of promise and deliver what everybody seemed to be demanding – that extra leap to Division Three? The answer was a definitive no. But not many could have thought just how awry their dreams would go on so many fronts in the months and years to come. The plunge from being one of non-League's elite was about to begin, despite the summer signing of Danny Bolt from Slough Town, which was seen then as the final piece in the jigsaw.

"There are some interesting times ahead", Davies had said on being re-elected chairman of the streamlined hierarchy. There was no question he was right on that score.

7

The Life of Brian
1998/99

John McGovern had the board of directors, led by chairman Jon Davies, believing he was the man to take Woking into the Football League. The Cards' hierarchy was flattered to be linked with a man who captained Derby County to a First Division Championship and then Nottingham Forest to two European Cup triumphs, together with a host of domestic honours. A man of principal, nurtured by the legendary Brian Clough, surely – after leading the team to a third-place finish in his first season – had the credentials to lead Woking into the promised land. However, the faith shown in the Scot by those who appointed him was hopelessly misguided.

When all is said and done, he was appointed despite his managerial record and not because of it, his reputation as a player going before him. Not only had Davies and his colleagues recruited a man who had achieved little at his previous clubs as a boss, they had hired a professional who had little or no knowledge of the non-League game. It took those in charge 15 months to realise their error, by which time the club was already on a downward slide from which it is still yet to recover.

McGovern had been appointed in the summer of 1997. But just eight matches into his second season – a period in which he had presided over six defeats – his reign came to an abrupt end. Incredibly, having had just one manager in 12 years up until McGovern's arrival, September 1998 was the month in which Woking were about to employ their third boss in little over a season.

Hednesford Town, Dover Athletic, Southport, Kettering Town and Kidderminster Harriers all had something in common. They had all beaten The Cards before August was up. The first point gained was at home to Forest Green Rovers but a week later a physical-but-uninspiring Barrow became the sixth team to inflict defeat on a demoralised side who had led 2-0 at half-time with goals from Richard Goddard and Steve West. A 3-2 reverse meant the writing was on the wall for McGovern, who stated after the match: "It's not difficult to imagine how I feel as a manager because I'm paid to get results and at the moment I'm not getting them." Ironically, he was to get his first win of the season in what turned out to be his last game in charge, at Leek Town on Saturday 12 September.

Danny Bolt, a £15,000 recruit, cracked home his first goal for the club after three minutes. Bolt's corner from the left five minutes later was headed on by transfer-listed Steve West and Michael Danzey stooped to head the second. West made it 3-0 after 25 minutes. That's the way it stayed but chairman Davies had barely been able to look McGovern in the eye before the match and it seemed the decision to dispense with the Scot's services had already been made.

Kevin Betsy receiving the 1997/98 player of the year award from the chairman, Jon Davies.

Normally accommodating with the press, albeit a little short with them on occasion, McGovern stormed straight past the waiting throng of reporters, out of the back door and on to the team coach without so much as a word. In his defence, his team had at last done the talking for him.

Apparently unbeknown to McGovern, moves were afoot to terminate his contract. Press officer Michael Church confirmed that a board meeting had already taken place two days before the Leek match but strangely it took those in charge three days to confirm their decision. That decisive meeting on Monday 12 September was followed by a press release the following afternoon at 3 p.m., just hours before The Cards were due to play Welling United. The statement was short and to the point, comprising just 51 words under the heading "John McGovern leaves Kingfield." Not a single word thanked him for his efforts at Kingfield and the man who ultimately had the responsibility of hiring him – Davies – was not in the mood to face the music and was unavailable for comment. McGovern was said to have been surprised by his fate, which was understandable in light of the fact he had just gained his first win of the season. But there were contributing factors.

The team's style of play – so entertaining under Geoff Chapple – had become stilted with little flair or imagination. There was talk of some players being told not to go over the halfway line or they would be fined. Apart from that, his own professionalism had been called into question when the team had arrived late at two away games in the four completed. He was reported to have set the leaving time for both. For his last game at

Grant Payne shielding the ball against Southport.

Leek it had been a 2.50 p.m. arrival at the ground, with the game eventually kicking off at 3.25 p.m. In any event, his dismissal would be a costly one for the club, with two years outstanding on a contract which is believed to have been paid off in instalments. To add insult to injury, McGovern – who lived in Sheffield and had been renting a houseboat on the Basingstoke Canal in West Byfleet during his Woking tenure – was alleged to have continued to drive his club sponsored car for a further 10 months. The sale of rising star Kevin Betsy to Kevin Keegan's Fulham coincided with McGovern's departure, with many fans suggesting that the £80,000 transfer fee received up front – with £75,000 to follow in instalments – was used to fund the pay off, an accusation denied by the club.

Skipper Andy Ellis, a stalwart who until that time had made around 180 appearances since his debut in 1994, took temporary charge of the team and the incredible thing about the match against Welling was that there were smiling faces at Kingfield again. It was as if a blanket of gloom had been lifted. Amid a strangely muted atmosphere, a 0-0 draw saw a second clean sheet and a spirited performance from the team. Ellis declared he did not really enjoy being in charge and he hoped that someone would be appointed before the match with Yeovil Town on the Saturday. The amiable Welshman got his wish.

The man in question was Brian McDermott, who most remember as being a bit-part player at Arsenal in the late 1970s and early '80s. He had gone on to make 300 Football League appearances with various clubs before becoming assistant manager at Yeovil Town. He then cut his teeth in management at Slough Town, where he spent

In the net – Steve West and Scott Steele against Barrow.

two-and-a-half years before financial problems at the club saw him sidelined from the game. At that time he was not only available, but on the Woking board's shortlist to take over on a trial basis. Bringing with him Kevin Hill, who made 95 appearances for The Cards in the 1980s, he accepted the position, met the staff and was at the helm for the visit of one of his former clubs.

McDermott was 37 years old and had an impressive CV, which included a UEFA Class A coaching badge – a qualification held by only five others in the country before him at the time of his appointment. He received a warm reception from a healthy attendance of 2,581 against Yeovil and the atmosphere at the club changed overnight to one of optimism. While the result was another 0-0 draw, the style of football was a joy to watch and McDermott had said of his first afternoon's work: "There was a lot of freedom in our play and we passed the ball around, held it up well and showed good skills". In his first team were: Laurence Batty, Brian Statham, Robin Taylor, Richard Goddard, Scott Smith, Michael Danzey, Danny Bolt, Andy Ellis (captain), Scott Steele, Steve West and Darran Hay. Between them they played the sort of football The Cards' fans had become accustomed to over the years – a style that had been stilted by McGovern. From the outset, McDermott was a hit.

There followed a 1-1 draw at eventual champions Cheltenham Town, in front of 3,406 at Whaddon Road, before McDermott, unbeaten in two matches, was rewarded with his first victory, a West hat-trick giving The Cards a 3-0 win at Northwich Victoria. "I didn't want to say anything before the game, but that's four wins and four clean sheets for me here," McDermott revealed afterwards. Had Woking found a lucky manager as well as a popular one?

It was a win that took Woking off the bottom of the Conference with ten points from 12 games – six of those points coming in the last four matches. Just two weeks before, West had been on the transfer list and had only one goal to his name. Now he was the toast of a team who had found a measure of resilience to go with a refreshing air of confidence. That confidence might have been dented by a 3-0 home defeat by Morecambe, but a magnificent 1-0 win at Doncaster Rovers, with West again the scorer, signalled a run of just a single defeat in the next 14 matches.

A 5-1 FA Cup win at Minehead, in which the prolific Hay netted four times, came the day after McDermott was handed a two-and-half year contract to succeed McGovern in the managerial hot-seat. The deal included a six-month severance clause for both parties – a legacy of the McGovern contract, which had no such stipulation. As it turned out, it was the manager and not the club who would ultimately benefit – but to a lesser degree by far than his predecessor. For now though, the grounding McDermott had enjoyed at Slough Town – a managerial period during which he had fallen just one hurdle short of Wembley in the FA Trophy – had prepared him for the challenge. He took it with both hands. Comparing life at the Wexham Park Stadium with Kingfield he commented:

Woking have a big reputation and there is a much bigger support. I looked around at Minehead when we were warming up and all I saw was red and white scarves. It made me feel proud to be part of it and that's how I feel about being here.

McDermott had made an immediate impression in the caretaker manager's role and now he was in the job for real. After a postponement against Telford just 15 minutes

Kevin Betsy strutting his stuff against Barrow.

before the kick-off, the next hurdle for the club could not have been bigger. Clashes with neighbours Aldershot Town had generally been confined to friendlies up until then. On Saturday 31 October hostilities resumed for real in the fourth qualifying round of the FA Cup. It attracted the biggest attendance for a qualifying-round tie in the competition for more than 30 years, with 6,870 at the Recreation Ground – despite monsoon conditions.

Having already paid £15,000 to Boreham Wood for left-back Rob Hollingdale four weeks previously, McDermott shelled out another £10,000 on elegant midfielder Steve Perkins from rivals Stevenage Borough. Perkins made his debut in what was a competitive, combative and passionate match dominated by the defences: New Zealand international Scott Smith illuminated the gloom with a faultless performance as sweeper and Eddie Saunders and Danzey provided the authority in the air.

The 0-0 scoreline guaranteed a bumper pay-day for Woking in the replay and McDermott was just pleased to be in the hat. Three days later, a magnificent goal from Steele gave The Cards a 2-1 extra-time triumph – their first win of the season at Kingfield at the eighth attempt. Gary Abbott had fired The Shots ahead before Hay equalised. Steele's moment of magic from the edge of the box gave McDermott another satisfying outcome in a match in which eight bookings (four each side) littered proceedings. Aldershot boss George Borg, one of the non-League game's more colourful characters, had once again tried and lost against Woking, as he had done on numerous occasions in the past as manager of Enfield. "I thought we were the better side over the two games but that's the cup," Borg told reporters. "Woking's players were shouting and

Danny Bolt was man of the match against Yeovil Town.

In need of help – Brian McDermott and Kevin Hill
at Northwich Victoria.

celebrating in the dressing room afterwards, which shows the respect they had for us. You don't expect to hear that from a Conference team at their place."

Cheltenham Town were next at Kingfield and McDermott's tactical awareness came to the fore as he masterminded a 1-0 victory, the first of eight wins in nine matches. The one defeat came at the hands of Third Division Scunthorpe United who ended The Cards' FA Cup adventure, the only goal coming from former Leeds United striker, Jamie Forrester. Incidentally, The Cards had never beaten a Football League side whose name begins with the letter 'S'. Scunthorpe joined Southend, Swindon and Swansea as conquerors of Woking in the FA Cup.

The draw for the FA Trophy – a more realistic chance of reaching the Twin Towers of Wembley – pitted Woking against Doc Martens League Premier strugglers Salisbury City. McDermott had gone on record as saying that his biggest personal disappointment in football had been when his Slough side had lost a two-legged semi-final against Southport seven months earlier. While Slough drew the second leg away at Haig Avenue, their home defeat in the first leg had been costly. That particular ground would return to haunt McDermott later during his Woking tenure, while Geoff Chapple's second spell in charge of The Cards also ended at what proved a managerial graveyard as far as the two men were concerned.

There was a scare against Salisbury City, with Woking lapsing into bad habits before goals from West and Ellis sent the club through to the third round. The visit of Hayes to Kingfield signalled The Cards' first home win of the season by a clear two goals and the club were slowly but surely rising from the depths of the Conference basement. It was a third successive league victory, among a barrage of cup ties. Significantly, there had been no goals conceded in that trio of triumphs. This was testament to the back three of Smith, Danzey and Saunders, together with 'keeper Batty, who was showing

Rob Hollingdale in action against Northwich Victoria.

top form since his return to the team – Darryl Flahavan having been custodian during the season's opening six matches.

Having started the campaign with a single point from 7 matches, Woking had now accumulated 19 from 16 and had climbed to fifteenth place, 5 points off the bottom three. McDermott was keen to play down rumours that The Shots' prolific marksman Abbott was about to join The Cards' ranks after a Grant Payne goal had brought about another win, this time at Welling United. "I was delighted with Grant and Westy up front and we have Darran Hay too," he insisted.

By now it was early December and, incredibly, the Conference Form League showed Woking at the summit with five victories and one defeat in their last six outings. That Stevenage Borough had been beaten into second place only seemed to add to the feeling of satisfaction for Woking supporters. In the same month McDermott signed another player from Broadhall Way when Phil Gridelet arrived on a free transfer. He was an ex-England semi-professional who had been voted Conference Player of the Year in 1991 while at Barnet, before a £175,000 move to Barnsley. He was now a Card after notching up around 200 appearances for Southend United (for whom he scored the winning goal against John McGovern's Woking in 1997/98). In the course of time he was not to be the most popular of players as far as the supporters were concerned and he later suffered the ignominy of being named in *Four Four Two* magazine's poll for the top 100 worst players of all time.

A Hay-inspired 2-1 win against Kidderminster Harriers at Kingfield saw Ladbrokes slash their odds on Woking lifting the league title from 100/1 to 40/1. It has to be said that those odds were not overly generous in the circumstances, with The Cards still looking a long way from being a championship-winning side. Nevertheless, win number

Darran Hay scores again and enjoys the adulation when The Cards played *v.* Northwich Victoria.

six in a row duly arrived and with it Woking's first double of the season. Northwich put up more resistance than when they were beaten 3-0 earlier in the season but goals from Steele (penalty) and the irrepressible Hay gave McDermott's buzzing team a 2-1 triumph. Hay and Steele both limped off, as did Gridelet, but it had still been a good day.

A noon kick-off at Kingstonian on Boxing Day, a fixture which had not featured on this particular date for 36 years, was not conducive to a feast of football as it turned out. A 0-0 draw against Geoff Chapple's Conference newcomers was about all Woking deserved and McDermott admitted: "We never came out for the second half and while we put a lot of effort in, like we always do, there wasn't enough quality. It's disappointing because I know we are a better team than that."

A trip to Rushden & Diamonds two days later saw the first league defeat since 3 October, but those who witnessed the clash at Nene Park would have marvelled at the football produced by the home team. The final scoreline was 2-0, but how Woking had managed to stay within one goal of Brian Talbot's side until the last minute was largely down to the agility of Batty. One save, a deflected volley from Jon Hamsher, saw the 'keeper arch back in an instant to somehow tip the ball over the bar. A later effort, when Miquel De Souza's header looked to have beaten him, could only be described in the same context as the best save of all – that of Gordon Banks from Pele in the 1970 World Cup.

But despite the heroics from Batty, Woking hit the buffers before the turn of the year and when Chapple returned to Kingfield for the first time as a visiting manager on New Year's Day, Kingstonian added to the woe with a 1-0 win. From a position where three holiday victories might have produced a top-three place, the reality of one point in nine was hugely disappointing.

Grant Payne has just scored a cracker against Rushden & Diamonds.

It was to get worse for McDermott and Woking as Telford recorded their first win in three months and only their fifth in 24 league matches in the season. "It's alright when you're winning six on the trot", said the frustrated boss. "But it's when you lose two or three and you have to battle, that's when you find out about the character of some players. Today was about us not wanting it as much as them and that hurt me."

In the next six matches, five were in either the Surrey Senior Cup or the FA Trophy. In the former, Epsom & Ewell and then Walton & Hersham were despatched with eight goals for and none conceded. But it was the Trophy that provided the real entertainment when an astonishing third-round home meeting with Folkestone Invicta ended 8-4 in The Cards' favour. What a thrill-a-minute contest it was. Statisticians claimed it was only the second time since the war that 12 goals had been scored at Kingfield in a competitive match while Hay's fourth goal was his 100th in a Cards shirt. Without realising it at the time, a little under 2,000 people had witnessed history in the making at Kingfield as Hay became the first man to score four goals in an FA Cup tie and FA Trophy match in the same season.

The amiable striker had achieved his ton in just 204 appearances, 42 of those as a substitute – all the more impressive when you consider that former boss Chapple's substitutions were generally reserved for the final few minutes of a match. Hay tried hard to play down his achievement but said afterwards: "I never imagined that I'd score my 100th goal today. This club is my life and it means so much to me." McDermott paid his own tribute by saying: "We are all delighted for Darran. For someone to score 100 goals at a football club in this day and age is phenomenal and you've got to say it's a fantastic record." Apart from anything else, the goals helped Woking to the last thirty-two of what had become their favourite competition.

After league defeat against Farnborough Town, 2,788 turned up to watch the next round of the Trophy at home to Rushden & Diamonds, who had beaten Slough Town, so denying McDermott an emotional return to the club he had guided to the semi-final the previous year. A 0-0 draw at Kingfield was followed by a 2-1 victory at Nene Park, as unexpected as it was magnificent given the mauling Woking had received on the same ground only a matter of weeks before. After a poor run in the league it gave the team a welcome boost.

But, while wins against Leek and Yeovil improved the league form, McDermott was about to meet his nemesis in the Trophy against the team that had broken his heart the previous term. Southport should have been swept away on a tide of goals on home soil as Payne and Hay in particular had an off day. "We had enough chances to win three games, let alone one", rued McDermott. "Not just half chances but clear cut ones and we haven't hit the target."

Seven other clubs had booked their place in the last sixteen – and it was to be Southport who joined them after a Dave Gamble penalty was enough to send them through in the replay on Lancashire's coastline. McDermott was devastated. "It's the second time I've come here and got turned over so I'm not a lover of the place," he groaned.

March 1999 was significant in that, for the first time, the public were becoming aware of Woking's financial problems. Gates were down, with little TV interest after two early exits in the FA Cup and during the fourteen-month period to July 1998, trading income relating to football activities was down by about half that of the previous year. A suggestion that £350,000 was the figure lost was played down by then financial director Bill Sutton, who commented: "The loss is historical and included six summer months, which distorts the figures. The loss also included the cost of converting the club to a limited company which was £70,000 and if you take away that figure it is not as bad as it looks."

The fact was that up until 1997 money had rolled in off the back of FA Cup and FA Trophy success. Since then, crowds had dropped significantly, the players wage bill remained high and having not capitalised commercially in the good times, the club were about to find out that operating while almost entirely reliant on gate receipts was a risky business.

Back on the pitch, Batty chalked up 400 appearances for The Cards in a 0-0 draw against Kettering Town and the 35-year-old commented:

When I came to Woking I wanted to achieve promotion, play in an FA Trophy final and play for my country. I've done all three and after eight years here I still love the club. I've got at least two good years left in me and I would love to finish my career with Woking.

Woking's sojourns in the cup competitions had already ended for another season, with Farnborough having put paid to their chances in the Endsleigh Challenge Trophy and

Stuart Girdler amid the fray against Rushden & Diamonds.

Darran Hay with his admirers.

Sutton United hammering them out of the Surrey Senior Cup in a humiliating 6-0 defeat. To add insult to injury, Saunders scored not one but two own goals: Steady Eddie was anything but that night. For the rest of the season the only thing to play for was mid-table respectability which, given the start to the campaign, was more than any Woking supporter could have hoped for.

A first ever defeat at home to Stevenage Borough was not a welcome one as far as Woking fans were concerned and losing Scott Smith, sent off after seven minutes for a professional foul, hardly helped the cause. A crowd of 2,776 saw the Hertfordshire outfit claim a 2-1 victory – their first in seven matches under Richard Hill. A win against Hednesford Town was tempered by the lowest crowd in the league that season. Only 1,453 chose The Cards over the full international that England was playing against Poland at the time. "We are going to announce the crowd changes to the team," quipped ground and safety officer Mike Bidmead before the match as 600 regulars stayed away. It highlighted once again the precarious plight of the club's finances with around £5,000 lost in gate receipts. At the time it was money the club could ill-afford to lose.

The Football Association were contacted by the officials of many Conference clubs voicing their concern at the loss in revenue, but Cards football director Phil Ledger confirmed that the FA had categorically refused to pay out compensation. A subsequent win against Hereford was not enough to heal some of the bruises – in Ledger's case, literally, following a fall on the team coach when the driver had suddenly braked.

Following a 0-0 draw at Southport, Hay receiving a red card, something extraordinary happened – Woking found themselves ninth in the league table. They would make it to seventh later. Finding The Cards on the top page on Teletext rather than the second half was disorientating at first. Meanwhile, McDermott was busy re-signing players. Steele, Scott Smith, Saunders and Batty had already put pen to paper on new deals while West, Danzey, Gridelet, Ben Kamara and Steve French were all due for talks with the boss. Favourite Dave Timothy was allowed to join Hampton.

A derby clash against Farnborough Town, totally devoid of passion, saw Rob Hollingdale get the sponsors' man of the match vote despite being on the pitch for only 44 minutes. The match saw the welcome return of Lloyd Wye to Kingfield, albeit playing for the opposition. Hollingdale scored his first goal for Woking and commented:

I'm normally a two or three goal a year man but I was beginning to think I wouldn't score this season. I feel like I'm playing well again after a dodgy spell following injury. Brian has encouraged me to take people on, which I'm enjoying.

A 5-0 thrashing at the hands of Stevenage at Broadhall Way was a big blow, but wins against Telford United and Barrow meant a seventh-place spot until defeat at home to Hereford on the last day of the season dictated a finishing position of ninth. In many ways it had been a traumatic season, both on and off the pitch, but despite that last day defeat, the overriding factor was one of relief that McDermott had turned around the club's fortunes after a dreadful start.

Off the pitch, the poor financial state of the club was beginning to rear its ugly head, while 100 years of tradition was brought to a close as Kingfield's twelve-man committee finally handed the reigns over to the new limited companies which would take their place. Woking were no longer a members club but were to be known as Woking Football Club (Holdings) Ltd – the freehold kept separately to the football activities – and Woking Football Club Ltd – the trading arm of the club. Seven directors were appointed: Davies, Church, Ledger, Sutton, Paul Elmer, Graham Elmer and John Taylor. "It was a decision that had to be made in order for us to pursue our aim of getting into the Football League," said Davies.

Little did the chairman know that his vision of promotion, and desire to take Woking forward, was as far away from reality as it was possible to be. And even those colleagues closest to him could not have envisaged that two months after outlining the club's future he would walk into a meeting of directors and stun them with his letter of resignation.

8

The Dark Days
1999/20

Those who thought that the threat of relegation from the Conference the previous season was a mere blip in the Woking history book were about to be proved wrong. This season will go down as one of the blackest in memory for many reasons. The football was merely incidental, a subplot running alongside the real story, bubbling under the surface. Boardroom upheaval, shareholder discontent, anarchy among supporters, another managerial sacking and financial mayhem were the orders of the day.

Yet optimism in the summer of 1999 was high and the trauma of John McGovern's departure and Brian McDermott's appointment appeared to have been forgotten, with McDermott showing signs of being the man to take on chairman Jon Davies' dream of taking the club forward. Up until ten months before, the relegation word had been alien to Woking fans and while reaching the Football League might have been a touch ambitious for the coming term, McDermott had managed to keep the majority of his squad. Moreover, he had proved himself adept at signings, introducing four new players – without paying out a penny in transfer fees. Long before a ball had been kicked in anger, however, in fact even before the first cross-country run had been initiated in pre-season training, the club was hit with a bombshell.

Chairman Davies, 47, walked into a board meeting just 24 hours before the players were due to report after their summer break and handed in his letter of resignation. The official reason given was because of increased work commitments but it was clear that he had been under pressure from some quarters to go – which went a long way to explaining the baffling timing of his decision. His fellow directors remained tight-lipped and one of them, Paul Elmer, voiced the view of the others by saying: "Jon has resigned due to business interests and that is what is in the club's statement. There is nothing else I can add." Elmer couldn't add what everybody else knew, that Davies had had enough grief from people in and around the club and could not face it any more.

Certain factions were expressing their dismay at the direction the club was headed. There had been suggestions of unrest among the shareholders and shortly before, at one of their meetings, an agreement was made to issue a request to the board demanding the resignation of four of the seven directors – including the chairman.

Davies, the boss of a local printing firm, is also understood to have received criticism from supporters, one of whom had had a letter published towards the end of the previous season attacking him personally for the way he was running the club. With the McGovern episode also having taken its toll, it was clear that matters had come to a head for a man who had been at the helm for two years, as well as being on the old

The Woking squad before the new season.

management committee for five years. As a supporter of the club for many seasons, it was a sad end for the local businessman.

McDermott was adamant that the chairman's departure would not affect matters on the pitch, which was all he was concerned with. Little did he know that in the next three months matters off the pitch would seriously affect the playing side with one of his best players, Grant Payne, sold to help pay the monthly wage bill. But at the time life was sweet for the manager. Having persuaded Michael Danzey, a £15,000 signing from Aylesbury, to sign a new two-year contract to stay at Kingfield in the summer, rather than join Rushden & Diamonds, McDermott was on a roll. He brought in four players to supplement a side that had finished ninth the previous season and former Woking councillor and long-time supporter David Mitchell commented: "I hope Jon Davies leaving is not going to destabilise anything because, on the playing side, I think things are looking good for the coming season." Even Barry Kimber, the club's legendary physiotherapist since 1974, was moved to say that this Woking squad was the strongest he had known in his time at Woking.

The reason for the optimism was the arrival of the quartet of new recruits. French striker Nassim Akrour had caused a furore at his club Sutton United after turning his back on Gander Green Lane to become a Card. Up until May 1999, he had been influential in firing Sutton to the Ryman League Premier Division championship with 32 goals and, contrary to reports, he was out of contract and arrived at Kingfield for nothing. Having supposedly not left Woking's Surrey rivals on the best of terms, it promised to add spice to the clubs' forthcoming Conference meetings.

Midfield battler Darron Wilkinson arrived from Hayes, again on a Bosman transfer, while right-back Peter Smith stepped down from Third Division football with Brighton & Hove Albion to sign for McDermott. Rob Smith, signed on a non-contract basis, made up the foursome. The former Yeovil defender was a gamble, given that this was his first pre-season in three years after suffering cruciate ligament injuries to both knees.

Meanwhile, off the field, Bill Sutton, the club's financial director, reluctantly agreed to accept the temporary role as chairman. And although John Taylor, Graham Elmer and Michael Church had been named as the three other directors the shareholders wanted to stand down, all refused to do so. "I will not be resigning, in fact the whole thing has made me more determined to carry on," said Church. Sutton was equally defiant and added:

I can confirm that there is a dissident group who have asked for the removal of certain directors. The board has decided to take this request as an attack against the whole board rather than the four who were named. One of them, Jon Davies, has resigned for his own reasons and that leaves six duly elected members who are happy with their own agenda. We will continue to fight as one until we are no longer elected.

The irony was that in the early 1990s, Sutton was criticised for trying to run the club in a more business-like fashion before he was reminded that it was a football club. Now the so-called dissident group were demanding that the business side was improved and Sutton added:

The four musketeers – Woking strikers Nassim Akrour, Steve West, Darran Hay and Grant Payne.

Phil Gridelet on show against Welling United.

The level of income in my view cannot be disassociated with the product and the product is what you see on the pitch. It forms the basis of getting people to part with their money. If that product is superb you will find it much easier to attract big sponsors, to maximise shop sales, to obtain match sponsorship and get people to pay for advertising boards. That will all come from success on the pitch but, because in the past two years we haven't been so successful, the whole level of income has dropped. It's far easier for income to slow down than for expenditure to do the same.

Many football clubs in the following few years would find that Sutton's words were profound – with the collapse of ITV Digital causing many Football League outfits to go into administration.

On the pitch, a so-called friendly at Worthing ended in a physical battle and a 2-2 draw, with the Woking players thankfully still in one piece afterwards. Then Laurence Batty enjoyed a bumper testimonial pay day against his former employers Fulham – with Danzey and the visitors' striker Barry Hayles both sent off, despite the game's friendly tag.

The first league game dawned and all eyes were on the new-look Cards as they headed to Southport for the opening day of the season. Woking had never beaten the Lancashire club on their own patch in six previous league attempts, while the memory of FA Trophy defeat in March was still very much to the forefront of people's minds. Nevertheless, McDermott was set to give four debuts to his new signings and he had

Rob Hollingdale on a surge.

the luxury of having four quality strikers in Akrour, Payne, Darran Hay and Steve West available to him. As it turned out it was defensively where his team let him down in a 4-1 defeat that made a mockery of the bookies' 10/1 odds for Woking to lift the Conference Championship.

A shell-shocked McDermott could not believe what he had just witnessed. "Defensively we were shocking", he said. "For a side that I put out there I am not happy. Southport outfought us in the midfield areas and one or two of their players bossed ours. It's something we're going to have to put right quickly." They were honest words. He had picked what would have been most people's starting eleven given the encouraging pre-season performances.

Three sendings off, including Eddie Saunders for Woking, and five bookings were a feature of Woking's first home match of the season, a 1-1 draw against Kettering Town in front of a healthy Tuesday night crowd of 2,205. But rather than stay with what he felt was his best team after the opening-day defeat, McDermott made what many people feel was his first mistake. While bringing in Scott Smith for Rob Smith was understandable, leaving out Scott Steele and Steve Perkins – the flair in the team – together with Grant Payne, was seen as a negative response to the Southport debacle which, in hindsight, should have been viewed as a one-off. The poor entertainment served up against Kettering was inevitable.

By the time Woking had lost 3-1 at home to Doncaster Rovers five days later, the air of optimism was in danger of being engulfed before the season had got going. Creative flair had again been passed over by McDermott and following a 40-minute inquest after the final whistle, he emerged to say:

Frenchman Nassim Akrour shows how it's done in his homeland.

If Steele and Perkins want the shirt it's there for them. If Danny Bolt wants it, it's there. But none of them are really taking it and I don't care who plays. It's up to them to show me in training and in games that they're worth a run in the side.

Both Perkins and Steele were in the team that picked up the first three points of the season at Welling United, before a Bank Holiday weekend which took in games away at Kidderminster Harriers and at home to Colin Lippiatt's Yeovil Town.

Once again there was a feeling of incredulity in the first of those encounters, a 3-2 reverse against a young and inexperienced Kiddie side still coming to terms with their self-belief after four straight defeats. Just how Woking contrived to lose a contest they dominated eluded all those who saw it. A Hay goal in the 85th minute looked to have rescued a point for The Cards, who just could not capitalise on their superior possession. But a slip from Saunders let in Dean Bennett, who bore down on Batty's goal before unleashing a shot from the edge of the box which flew into the bottom corner.

Batty was the latest scapegoat and from then on lost his place in goal to Darryl Flahavan – custodian for the next nine outings, beginning with the game against Yeovil. Saunders was also left out against Lippiatt's high-flyers, with centre forward West preferred in defence. It was to prove an inspired switch and the former Enfield striker later went on to win international honours as a centre-back. Payne was brought in for the luckless Akrour who, despite some nice touches, had not looked like scoring during his first taste of Conference football.

Scott Smith signs on the dotted line.

Only Peter Smith of the new summer recruits was in the starting line-up to face The Glovers, with Hay and West scoring the goals in a 2-0 win – the first home victory of the campaign against a side that included former Cards' hero Kevan Brown. Previously allowed to leave Kingfield before his time, Brown was destined to make an emotional return to The Cards before the season was out. The topsy-turvy results continued with a home defeat against Hednesford Town, before a magnificent 3-1 triumph at Rushden & Diamonds. The match at Nene Park was significant in that Akrour grabbed his first goal for Woking in six starts, having been rested for two games. It was a tremendous team performance and McDermott enthused: "We really played some nice stuff in the second half and we are delighted with the way the lads performed. We've come to a top club and thoroughly deserved to win the three points."

While there had been an upturn of sorts on the pitch, off it the board of directors had called an extraordinary meeting asking for a vote of confidence from the shareholders. With a margin of 45-23 in the directors' favour, with two abstentions, the long-running saga had been brought to an end with those shareholders declaring their faith in the six men who were running the club. A 'constructive' discussion replaced the usually more heated debates, with Sutton putting forward the board's objectives on the commercial side. Leading spokesman for the so-called 'dissident group' Peter Jordan admitted:

It was the best conducted meeting I've ever been to at Woking Football Club. We have voiced our opinion and we believe the directors have taken our comments on board.

We have caused some waves but we feel we have done some good as we have highlighted issues that need to be addressed. We have offered our help and they have agreed to listen to our suggestions. We now back them 100 per cent.

Former Mayor of Woking and committee member Terry Molloy, another leading spokesmen for the dissenters, added: "There was give and take on both sides and a feel-good conclusion to the meeting. I'm very much more confident and happy about matters off the pitch now than prior to the meeting."

Sutton came through with real credit for appeasing those men who were against the board, while there was a sense that the shareholders too had benefited as they had pointed out areas for concern and were willing to help out for the good of the club.

Back to the football and a 1-1 draw at Altrincham, with Hay scoring his fourth goal in five starts, saw Woking manage to go two consecutive matches without losing, for the first time since the start of the season. Phil Gridelet become as prolific on the yellow card front as Hay had with his goals. In what was an ill-tempered meeting at Moss Lane, the midfielder added to his tally of three yellows in five games with another two – to receive his marching orders after 65 minutes. "When you are down to ten men and you are playing up north, if you get a point you take it," said McDermott. But with only 11 points to show from 9 matches, it was hardly a start to set the league alight and Woking hovered above the usual bottom-of-the-table suspects: Dover, Welling, Telford, Sutton, Hayes and Forest Green Rovers.

Heavy rain put paid to the home fixture with Northwich Victoria and highlighted the poor drainage at Kingfield. More to the point, with income so heavily dependant on

Handbags aplenty against rivals Aldershot Town.

gate receipts, the abandonment had a serious impact on the club's cash-flow, with no home game between 4 September and 9 October. "It never helps to have games postponed," said Sutton, who was continuing to double up as chairman and financial director. "It usually means the game is rearranged later in the season on a Tuesday night and historically our gates are not as good in midweek," he added.

The drainage problem had only come to light since the Leslie Gosden Stand was constructed. "The water has nowhere to go and we had a radar survey done last year which identified bone-hard ground 2ft under the pitch," Sutton explained, before confirming that it would take around £25,000 to fix the problem. The directors considered it but at the time it was an expense they felt the club could ill-afford.

When 9 October came around, a 2-0 home defeat to Hereford United, which saw The Cards plummet into the bottom three, was not the ideal preparation for an FA Cup fourth qualifying round tie at home to Doc Martens League Premier Division side Burton Albion. They were a club on the up with a certain Nigel Clough in charge and this term had lost just one competitive match – on the opening day of the season. But Woking were the favourites and in desperate need of a cup run to generate finances – something that had been commonplace in the 1990s. The Kingfield faithful, used to dining out on an à-la-carte menu in the cup in recent years, were treated to mere scraps from the table as their side scratched around with little imagination in a 1-1 draw. Payne's exquisite goal was all Woking had to show for their efforts.

The headline, "Gone for a Burton" seemed to have an inevitability about it before a ball was kicked in the replay and so it was that in front of a partisan crowd at Eton Park, The Cards were beaten 3-1 after extra time. The result did not tell the whole story though, with Hay missing a penalty and Peter Smith being sent off after 77 minutes. Cards' skipper Danzey reflected the mood of his team by saying: "We played the better football but didn't take our chances. The game hinged on two incidents and I feel the players have let Brian (McDermott) down."

The impact was immediate and a crowd of just 1,505 – a figure hardly seen on a Saturday since the club's Ryman League days – had serious implications on the budget once more. McDermott admitted to feeling the pressure even at that early stage of the season but he insisted: "It's a long-term objective here and if you change your manager twice in a year that's not good news." Rumours that Payne was to be transferred to rivals Aldershot Town were quashed by football director Phil Ledger and the striker was instrumental in ensuring Woking did not drop to the bottom rung of the Conference, scoring in a 2-1 win at home to fellow strugglers Forest Green Rovers. In addition the fans had been entertained in a match where Steele was only introduced as a second half substitute. The roar at the final whistle prompted McDermott to say afterwards: "I've told the players the season starts here".

Meanwhile, Taylor received the unanimous vote among his boardroom colleagues to assume the role of chairman of the club. The 57-year-old former vice-chairman (and a committee member for the previous twelve years), promised a new approach and was prepared to tackle the off-the-field problems head on. Many considered him a brave man to take on a job that had become a poisoned chalice. Sutton was relieved to relinquish the role and he was the first to admit that a collar and tie was not his style.

Steve Perkins on duty at Haig Avenue, Southport – a Woking manager's graveyard.

The new incumbent appeared 'Taylor-made' for the position and spoke of "building bridges" with the dissenters to "get them on our side". One of those men, Jordan, was voted onto the board of Woking Football Club (Holdings) Ltd and this was seen as the first step to appease the shareholders. Talk of raising funds by way of a share issue was mooted and Jordan was given responsibility for fundraising. Taylor attempted to play down the worsening financial position by saying: "I wouldn't say it's particularly brilliant but we're okay". In fact it was far from that and while the dust settled between directors and dissenters, there was no getting away from the fact that a very large problem was looming. Being knocked out of the FA Cup had not helped and, as well as the prize money being forfeited, gates for the following three home matches were only marginally better than 1,500. Then came another bolt from the blue.

Payne, one of the few flair players in the Woking set-up, was sold to George Borg's Aldershot Town against the wishes of both himself and boss McDermott. The transfer fee was £20,000, which most people associated with the club thought was derisory. Worse still, it told the world that Woking had to sell to survive and they were willing to give away players on the cheap – even to their closest rivals. Had it been a legal battle concerning the credibility of Woking's ambition to gain Football League status, the case for the defence would have been laughed out of court.

The transfer went down like a lead balloon among supporters and highlighted just how bleak things were at Kingfield, with Taylor admitting: "It's a matter of mathematics and the finances aren't good at the moment. It's serious but I can't say how serious." The press release had stated: "The board would like the fans to know that the sale was done reluctantly". The fact was that the alarming drop in attendance had finally taken its toll and Payne was made the sacrificial lamb in order for players' monthly wage bill to be met. McDermott was gutted: "When Grant came into my office his face was like mine. He was genuinely upset and so was I."

"It's a quick fix", added Taylor. "It was done for a cash injection and Grant was the only player anyone showed any interest in. It's not the sort of message we want to send out because nobody wants to get rid of their best players." Too late. While the extent of the problem was not revealed, it did not take a magician to work out the club were haemorrhaging money at around £4,000 a week.

After Payne had scored four goals against Enfield on his Shots' debut, just two days after waving goodbye to the club he loved, Andy Turner, a long-term supporter who later went on to be the club's tannoy announcer, spoke for the fans by saying:

George Borg must be laughing all the way to the bank. For the club to sell one of its better assets for such a small amount beggars belief. It puts us over in a very bad light and pours scorn on the statement that we are a progressive club. We are yesterday's club and I'm afraid the likes of Burton Albion and Aldershot are waiting in the wings to take our place.

Taylor must have wondered what he had let himself in for. Just four weeks after taking the chairmanship, a home defeat against Welling United was followed by a group of around twenty supporters forcing their way into the boardroom half-an-hour after the match. Damage was done to the door and shocked directors agreed to a meeting

On-loan defender Barry Miller and colleagues prepare for the action ahead.

with the fans on the following Thursday: a lack of communication between both parties had always been a bone of contention with those who handed over hard-earned money to come through the turnstiles.

The meeting did much to clear the air, with Sutton, now able to concentrate solely on financial matters, quick to point out:

This wasn't the board that lost £250,000 in 1994 and not the board which saw the benefit of what Geoff Chapple's teams managed to achieve. This is a board that has presided over three years of underachievement on the pitch.

With Sutton seeming to be very slow at getting audited accounts organised, all that could be gleaned was that a loss of around £200,000 was predicted for the year ending July 1999, with a similar deficit for 2000, although the reality in both cases was a loss slightly less than anticipated. Simon People, a Woking supporter both home and away for fifteen years, commented: "The directors are at last taking notice of the fans. It's been a long time coming but it's nice to see."

Meanwhile, form in the league continued in similar vein, with the only bright moment being a 1-0 victory at Stevenage Borough on 18 December, thanks to a West goal which barely crossed the line. It was the first league win in almost two months.

The next triumph came at Kingstonian on Boxing Day, but in the meantime The Cards had quietly progressed in the FA Trophy with wins against Ashford Town and Whyteleafe – setting up a much welcomed fourth-round clash with none other

Scott Steele has just scored a crucial penalty against Kidderminster Harriers.

than Aldershot Town, Grant Payne and all. In terms of a money-spinner, Sutton could not have picked a better draw if he had been pulling the balls out of the hat himself.

Close on 5,000 people saw a 0-0 draw at Kingfield, but a 2-0 home league reverse against Stevenage Borough was hardly ideal preparation for the replay. Relegation was a word that sent a shiver down the spine but the way in which McDermott's team threw in the towel against their old foe brought home just how real the possibility was. Little did McDermott know at the time but he would have just four more matches in charge and it seemed it was only the FA Trophy run that was preventing the directors saying, "Thanks for your efforts Brian but no thanks".

A Hay goal in front of 5,524 paying customers at The Recreation Ground, with the evening marred by a kung-fu-style assault by Aldershot's Jimmy Sugrue on Wilkinson, saw a pulsating contest end with a 1-0 victory for The Cards. In hindsight it only served to prolong McDermott's agony in a season which had turned horribly wrong for an amiable man. He had admitted that the previous four days, since the Stevenage defeat, had been horrendous for him and that this subsequent result was thanks to his players having, "big hearts." It proved only temporary respite.

The home clash with Altrincham was another disastrous day, a 1-0 defeat sparking fresh speculation that the boss' time was up. It was February, the club were still in the bottom three and the match was significant in that skipper Danzey damaged knee ligaments, which would ultimately force his retirement from football. Still the directors showed their blind faith in McDermott simply because the club were still in the FA Trophy. A Surrey Senior Cup win against Crystal Palace did nothing to help his

It's all over – The Cards win at Yeovil Town to confirm their Conference status.

The players acknowledge the jubilant supporters who made up the trip to Huish Park.

cause before a last throw of the dice came his way on 26 February. How ironic that the last-sixteen FA Trophy clash should be at probably the only place McDermott wanted to avoid at all costs. Another dreaded trip to Southport and Haig Avenue loomed. A comprehensive 3-0 defeat, with his team bereft of ideas, spelt the end. Even defender Richard Goddard had been tried up front to show just how desperate McDermott's thinking had become.

The inevitable sacking came following a Monday board meeting, leaving Woking's new skipper West admitting: "There are a lot of players who haven't really dug in for Brian. I'm gutted for him. But the dressing room is a bit dead and we need someone to liven it up." That someone was a familiar name. Colin Lippiatt breezed into Kingfield in his inimitable, larger-than-life fashion, got the smiles on faces and a 2-1 win at Telford United in his first match in charge. Many had thought his return would be with Chapple and it later transpired that the plan was for Lippiatt to keep the seat warm for when Chapple would join him in the summer.

There is no doubting Lippiatt's influence saved the club from a calamitous fate and, bearing in mind he had just two months to save his beloved Woking, his achievement in doing so was nothing short of a miracle. He brought in Barry Miller and Julian Charles on loan, while former hero Kevan Brown, Matt Hayfield and Steve Stott were signed from Lippiatt's former club Yeovil Town. The signings were as inspired as they were needed but successive home defeats against Hayes and Sutton United, in a run of just 7 points from 27, culminated in a 3-1 reverse at Northwich. It left Woking second from bottom and 6 points adrift of Kettering Town who were three places above them.

A 1-0 win at Nuneaton Borough, with Hay again on target, was the start of an incredible five-match-winning run that defied belief. Steele's 68th minute penalty at home to Telford United on 24 April brought about the first home league win for six months and edged The Cards out of the bottom three above Welling, Forest Green and Sutton – The U's being doomed. Then, not content with that, Steele was on target again against Kidderminster Harriers as another 1-0 triumph signalled a hat-trick of wins – with Harriers still clinching the league title on the same day because of Rushden & Diamonds' shortcomings.

Just 48 hours later, goal difference, games in hand and safety margins were all rendered academic on a glorious Bank Holiday Monday in Somerset when goals from Akrour, Hay and Hayfield secured a 3-0 win at Yeovil and with it continued Conference status. How fitting that Lippiatt should achieve his mission against his former club at Huish Park, with a magnificent visiting support there to witness events. Just for good measure, The Cards beat Dover 2-0 at Kingfield – before losing to Scarborough on the final day. Neither result mattered.

There was huge relief that The Cards were safe. Astonishingly, the club had picked up more than a quarter of their season's points tally in two weeks to finish in fourteenth place, with Altrincham and Welling joining Sutton as the relegated clubs. The consensus of opinion will always be that, but for Lippiatt and his signings, Woking would surely have been among them.

9

Saving the Best Until Last
2000/01

On reflection, just how Woking had managed to escape relegation the previous season was a feat of Houdiniesque proportions. A club that could not win at home for six months suddenly won three times at Kingfield in the space of ten days. The away form was also key, with wins at Welling, Rushden, Stevenage, Kingstonian, Telford, Hereford and Yeovil. Without those travelling triumphs the conclusion to Woking's season would have been over by Easter, let alone May. Colin Lippiatt rightly got the praise for returning as the prodigal son and saving The Cards with his unique blend of exuberance and humour. His knowledge of the right contacts at the right time also proved crucial. He was fortuitous in that his old club Yeovil were discarding players who did not want to go full-time, but you make your own luck and Lippiatt had managed to persuade the likes of Matt Hayfield, Steve Stott and Kevan Brown to join in the battle to save Woking from the dreaded drop. The loan signing of Barry Miller was also pivotal.

Having had a stab at management on his own at Yeovil, Lippiatt had enjoyed his second spell in sole charge of a Nationwide Conference outfit. So much so that the rumours of Chapple joining him in the summer never materialised, amid suggestions that the new boss had done a U-turn on his verbal agreement with his old ally. Chapple was still very much in charge at Kingstonian and The Cards could never have afforded to pay the remaining years on his contract to lure him back. But gossip had it that Chapple was unhappy at K's and was prepared to return to his beloved Woking, although publicly the former Kingfield legend swore his allegiance to Kingstonian and said that he would honour his contract with them. Whatever the real story, Chapple consoled himself with his fifth FA Trophy triumph in seven years at Kingsmeadow.

In the close season, Lippiatt had wasted no time in discarding Stott, Eddie Saunders, Rob Smith, Danny Bolt and Stuart Girdler, while Laurence Batty and Darran Hay were both offered contracts they felt unable to accept. Darryl Flahavan and Nassim Akrour wanted League football. Rather than re-sign for Woking, Akrour decided to tout himself to anybody interested and while he was reported to have trials with Brentford and Stoke City, he was prepared to return to Kingfield later in the summer with his tail between his legs. Football director Ledger confirmed: "Nassim's agent rang and asked if we could take him back". However, there was no room in the budget and the striker was given a firm, "no". Hay was "devastated" to be told by Lippiatt to look for another club after his one-year contract offer was revised in line with the board's new budget. The striker had written himself into Woking folklore with 124 goals in 271 appearances, 53 as a substitute. When he did find a club it was not the most popular move among

Charlie Griffin and Steve Perkins at arm's length against Hednesford Town.

Cards' fans – he joined Paul Fairclough at Stevenage Borough. This came after he had previously been rumoured to say: "I'd rather stick pins in my eyes than join Stevenage".

With the traumas of the previous season behind the club, mid-table respectability for the coming campaign would be considered a success. But secretly Lippiatt wanted a top-six finish to build on his achievements since his return. The question now was who would be the men to come in and revive Woking's fortunes? The answer, when it came, was complicated: the fortunes were hardly revived, and the men who came in were not destined to do anything that resembled reviving – with the exception of two. There were six new recruits, all signed under the Bosman ruling. Jamie Pitman, on a two-year deal, became the latest ex-Yeovil player to join his old boss. In 1998 Lippiatt had signed the 24-year-old for Yeovil from Hereford, where he had made 60 Football League appearances. Pitman would fill the right-wing back role and he was delighted to join The Cards. "Woking are a big club and every time I've played there the atmosphere has been great", he said. "I know Colin well and when he asked me to sign I had no hesitation. He's a manager I respect and is good with players."

Next in was Mark Watson, the second forward, after Akrour, to leave Sutton United for Kingfield in twelve months. The 26-year-old scored 11 times for the U's despite not gaining a regular place at Gander Green Lane and Lippiatt reasoned: "He will add physical presence up front and I hope he will improve our goals per games ratio which wasn't good enough last season."

The goalkeeping dilemma was solved, temporarily at least, by the recruitment of 24-year-old Mark Ormerod from Brighton & Hove Albion, where he had made 78 first-team appearances. His arrival meant the end for Batty, with Lippiatt insisting: "In the

Rob Hollingdale in the local clash against Kingstonian.

end I decided to go in a new direction. I'm paid to make decisions but this was the toughest I've had to make because Laurence and I go all the way back to the early 1980s." Little did the boss know that his new number one would cost him valuable points and earn himself the nickname 'Mark Oh My God'. He pulled the green jersey on just 10 times in the Conference.

Mark Druce from Kidderminster and Jae Martin from Peterborough United were also given two-year contracts, while Nick Roddis arrived on a non-contract basis from Hayes. In the main the signings were disastrous. Of the six newcomers only two lasted until the second half of the season, with Lippiatt admitting the error of his ways.

Meanwhile, off the pitch, a boardroom shake-up at the end of the previous season had seen John Taylor, Michael Church and Graham Elmer stand down, leaving only Phil Ledger, Bill Sutton and Paul Elmer of the original board remaining. At the club's AGM, they were joined by Peter Jordan, John Buchanan, Terry Molloy and David Mitchell, to restore the number of directors to seven.

"There are a lot of people wanting to get on the board and I felt it was time for someone younger to have a go," said 64-year-old Church. The commercial department gained a new commercial manager in Mick Hooker – but his appointment proved to be a poor addition to the team. Hooker talked a good game but he was another who failed to last the pace. In fact he was so anonymous in his dealings that many Cards' fans will not remember him ever being in the job. Of the new men on board at the helm, Molloy (68), was the unanimous choice as chairman and he promised to never again alienate the fans. The hostilities that had gone before had been a wake-up call for the directors and Molloy's opening gambit in his new role was a rallying cry. "First and foremost we want to maintain contact with our supporters and return to being a family club," he insisted. Molloy had been on the committee for two years in the 1970s and six years in the 1990s. He had now become the fourth chairman at the club in ten months. Buchanan became vice chairman, Mitchell company secretary and Jordan commercial director.

A new sponsorship deal with telepeople.com was signed and sealed – unlike the deal with previous sponsor MX, who failed to pay all the money owed because of alleged irregularities with the contract. Business acumen had not been high on the club's list of attributes at that time. With the new deal signed, things were looking up off the pitch.

As the season approached, Lippiatt was still not happy with the way his team was performing and his indecision with personnel soon became apparent. Not satisfied with the cover available in defence, with Scott Smith absent at the start of the season because of international commitments with New Zealand, Lippiatt signed Aiden O'Brien on a non-contract basis one week, only to change his mind about the player and release him a few days later. But on a budget that was "workable with a bit of wheeling and dealing," Lippiatt had done the best he could in the circumstances. Now it was time for action. One of his comments before the curtain-raiser smacked of classic understatement. "I don't want the supporters to get carried away or be under illusions about how tough it will be this year," he said. The only chance Cards' fans had of getting carried away was in a straightjacket – their sanity having been tested with two seasons of dross on the pitch.

Martin Randall punches the air in delight after scoring against Doncaster Rovers.

Lippiatt spoke of transitional periods, disciplined, attacking football and wanting a goal return in double figures from at least two of his strikers as well as a contribution of around eight goals from a midfield player. Wanting and getting proved to be two different things.

First match of the season and being up north had previously proved to be a combination hardly conducive to a Woking win. The previous season it had ended in a 4-1 defeat at Southport. This time it was a little further up the Lancashire coast at Morecambe. There were seven changes to the line-up of twelve months earlier, but it made no difference. Once again it was a three goal trouncing, this time with a 3-0 scoreline.

Ormerod had kept the score down against the Shrimps and was The Cards' player to emerge with the most credit on the day. But three days later, at home to Yeovil, the 'keeper was to bang the first nail in his own coffin. Roddis was brought in for Wilkinson, Watson for Druce and Scott Smith for youngster Richard Taylor, who had hardly put a foot wrong at Morecambe. Woking stormed into a 2-0 lead inside 11 minutes to stun Yeovil, managed by former Chelsea hero Dave Webb. The second goal was a tremendous strike from 25 yards by Watson and at that time Lippiatt's judgement on the striker appeared to be spot on. Then Ormerod spilled a cross under pressure to allow Barrington Belgrave to score and give The Glovers a lifeline. Early in the second half, Anthony Tonkin burst past Brown on the left before delivering a low shot towards the near post. Ormerod, half expecting the cross, let the ball crawl under his body as he tried to gather. It was 2-2 and if the ground had opened up at that moment the 'keeper would have been the first to dive into it – although he possibly might have missed, given his form on the night. Ben Smith's astonishing volley, after being set up by Warren Patmore, sealed Woking's fate and Lippiatt did not hold back afterwards, saying: "In my opinion we were the best side over the 90 minutes but unfortunately Mark (Ormerod) gift-wrapped them the three points". Failing to appreciate the irony, Lippiatt added: "He held his hand up to the goals but he cost us the game in my view".

Ormerod kept his place at home to Boston United five days later, an occasion when the man of the match was undoubtedly referee Steven Chittenden. He managed to chalk up seven yellow cards in 44 minutes but fortunately slowed down in the second half, finishing on just the ten. Watson showed the fallibility in front of goal which was to eventually cost him his place in the side and the contest ended in a 1-1 draw.

A Scott Steele penalty brought about Woking's first victory of the season at Doncaster Rovers. The amazing statistic to come from the contest was that in the previous eight seasons, Steele had never scored for Woking in a 1-0 win. There was every reason to feel optimistic when Hereford United were the next visitors to Kingfield – despite The Bulls not having conceded a goal on their travels in the opening month. A calamitous performance, with Ormerod again blundering to let in the visitors for their first goal, saw a 3-0 reverse which set alarm bells ringing with the season in its infancy. The fact that Watson and Martin were replaced after 56 minutes spoke volumes for Lippiatt's thoughts on two of his new strikers. He reserved his comments for his side's defending, however. "We conceded three cheap goals", he moaned;

The first was laughable in terms of this level of football. The second was a penalty and the third was like watching Sunday morning football and was men against boys. It was a struggle to find even three players who came anywhere near the standards I expect and that they should be setting themselves.

Lippiatt was forced to run an eighteen-man squad with the tight budget imposed. A defeat at Yeovil Town, to a Paul Steele goal, meant that The Cards had lost 6 of their first 7 outings and Lippiatt was already on the warpath and threatening to axe under-performing players.

Ben Wright, who two years later would help knock Chelsea out of the UEFA Cup while playing for a Norwegian club side, was drafted in as a loan signing from Bristol City for a 0-0 draw at Dover. Three days later, a paltry 1,139 crowd at Kingfield saw another poor showing, this time in a 2-1 defeat by Hayes. The Cards had just two efforts on goal all night and only had a Hayfield penalty to show for their efforts. With just 5 points from 8 matches, Woking were rock bottom of the league and the gulf in status was never more apparent than when top of the table Rushden & Diamonds completed a straightforward 4-1 success at Kingfield. Diamonds' Duane Darby and Justin Jackson cost £300,000 between them, while Lippiatt had had little option but to gamble on men that no-one else felt the need to sign – although he had made the mistake of offering longer-term deals than might have been expected for footballers he had barely seen play. The message from chairman Molloy was "don't panic" and while he expressed concern publicly, the thought of changing the manager again never entered his thinking.

Steve Perkins in the thick of it against his old club, Stevenage Borough.

Steve West defies the laws of gravity against Scarborough.

To do so would be unfair to Colin, the directors and the supporters. In the short time he's been here he has saved the club from certain relegation and what is important now is that we have some stability. It's not the answer to keep getting rid of the manager and we still believe we've got a chance with Colin and with the squad he's got.

While Lippiatt was campaigning for some flexibility with the budget, Molloy insisted:

We would love to spend the sort of money that Rushden have but to do so would mean the club being finished within a month. We don't want relegation of course, but spending money we haven't got would mean bankruptcy.

For his part Lippiatt added: "I will always retain my enthusiasm for the job. I knew it would be difficult when I first came but it's turned out to be harder than I imagined."

The manager declared he would make an analysis from week to week and put players on the transfer list in the hope of getting some out to bring in others. "The bottom line is we're not good enough," he maintained. Trying to raise morale while making statements about the lack of quality in the squad was Lippiatt's conundrum.

That Ormerod was the first to lose his place – he was destined to end up at Dorchester Town – was no great surprise. The return to Kingfield of Flahavan in his place was more of a shock, the 'keeper having been training at Southend United and Yeovil since leaving The Cards in the summer. Also in were Martin Randall from Hayes and former favourite Shane Wye, who signed Conference forms following his return from New Zealand. The midfielder was ready to try his luck at the club he still loved. Darron Wilkinson was offloaded to Slough Town on loan, a move that became permanent, and rumours persisted that Martin and Watson would be next to leave. The wheels were already set in motion for a change in fortunes – of sorts.

Flahavan, Wye and Randall were all in the team that beat Southport 1-0 at Haig Avenue. Chapple, McGovern and, in particular, McDermott had all tried and failed on this ground as Cards' managers. Lippiatt had become the first man to lead a winning team at The Sandgrounders' home since they joined non-League's elite in 1992. Woking had now won 2 in 10 matches, both of which were away. Significantly, skipper West pledged his future to Woking by signing a two-year extension to his contract which was up at the end of the season. It was a turning point. After the troubles of the previous year when Grant Payne was sold, it appeared as though Woking were determined to buck the trend and keep hold of their best players. "Maybe there were a few other clubs interested in me but I'm happy to stay and Colin wants me to stay," he said. "This is the club for me." At a time when players held the trump card over clubs, the negotiation of a hefty signing-on fee no doubt helped West make his decision.

The next two wins were both away from Kingfield, at Hednesford Town and Dagenham & Redbridge. The win at Keys Park saw The Cards rise to the heady heights of sixth from bottom of the Conference with 12 points from 13 matches. The next, at Victoria Road, saw the introduction of another loan signing – 21-year-old Charlie Griffin from Swindon Town. He had netted 30 goals for Screwfix League Chippenham Town two years before – a record that had prompted Swindon to fork out £10,000 for the striker. He netted the winner against The Daggers to begin his Woking career with a bang.

Having been delighted with the contribution from Flahavan, Lippiatt was faced with another goalkeeping crisis when Southend boss Dave Webb, who had moved to the

Steve West about to launch a shot on goal in typical style.

Essex club from Yeovil, came knocking for a player who was not on contract. Flahavan wanted League football. Everybody knew what the outcome would be and Lippiatt was facing up to losing the popular number one who had lasted just eight games on his return. Lippiatt wasted no time in recruiting a replacement. Basingstoke Town may not have been the obvious choice of club from which to plunder a Conference-standard stopper, but the Hampshire club were paid a fee of £4,000 for the services of Australian, Vince Matassa. The 6ft 3in former Aussie rules player was signed until the end of the season with an option for a further year. While some of Lippiatt's signings left a lot to be desired, there is no disputing that this was right up there with any bargain you would care to mention.

Matassa, 27, worked in Woking and Lippiatt enthused: "Vince has a great physique and a real physical presence about him in the way he commands his area. I think he has the potential to be better than the two we've already had this season."
At the same time the boss admitted that signing Martin and Druce had been a double error of judgement and both strikers were about to leave. Martin, having been banished to the reserves, had his contract terminated, while Druce was packed off to Oxford City on loan. Ormerod too was on his way to Dorchester Town.

A remarkable gesture from Woking's fans was made when members of the supporters club agreed to help fund Woking's non-contract players. Flahavan (until the time he left,) Roddis and Wye were among those who were being funded outside the strict wage structure incurred by the directors. Treasurer of the supporters club, Peter Mansell, commented: "There is a general feeling that the supporters want to help. Not everyone is happy with the situation but the supporters club does understand the restraints in place because of the financial position." Chairman Molloy was overwhelmed and got a little carried away when he added: "It's marvellous. The supporters association's gesture is a constructive move to involve themselves more closely with the club to ensure that hopefully we provide a squad that's vying for promotion in the future." Dream on was most people's reaction to that statement.

A light-hearted moment in the season then emerged, albeit downright embarrassing, when the club signed an imposter claiming to be Watford's Gifton Noel-Williams. He turned out to be no-one of the sort but Lippiatt and Ledger were hoodwinked into believing the scam and not only signed him, but sent his registration to the FA. "This chap came in a couple of weeks ago and said who he was and that he wanted to play for Woking. We signed him on Conference forms," recalled Ledger. When the player got cold feet the following day, the bizarre incident was concluded, but not before the 'news' was published in the weekly *Conference Bulletin* newsletter.

With Matassa making his debut and Griffin and Randall notching the goals, Woking at last gave the home fans a reminder of what it was like to win a match at Kingfield. It had been 171 days since the previous occasion – a 2-0 win against Dover Athletic in May. Now it was 21 October. An FA Cup fourth qualifying round victory over Hereford United followed but a league drubbing at Northwich, followed by a scrambled point at home to Leigh RMI, was not the best preparation for a trip to Cumbria to meet Carlisle United in the FA Cup first round. A change of formation to include a sweeper in a back five resulted in a shocking performance from Woking, indeed it was one of the worst

Matt Hayfield can't hide his delight after notching in the 4-4 draw at home to Dagenham & Redbridge.

in their FA Cup history. Carlisle, perennial strugglers at the foot of Division Three, would have thought that a win was beyond them. To achieve victory – scoring five goals in the process – was pure fantasy.

"There were a lot of basic things wrong with our shape but it's not about systems it's about players," said Lippiatt afterwards. What it was about was a lot of people who had risen from their beds at 6 a.m., travelled 650 miles and paid out good money to watch their team be humiliated. Lippiatt was hurting after the debacle but he went public in questioning whether his players had any mental strength. His criticism of his players was both public and stinging.

At the same time, Bill Sutton announced his decision to relinquish his position as a director of the club. Many people considered the former treasurer of the committee – and more recently financial director – to be the power behind the throne at Kingfield over the years and finding a man who would want to take on the thankless job of recording loss after loss on file was the next task. Sutton had been under pressure to bring the club's accounting procedures up to date, but showed a reluctance to put them on computer – essential for a business with a turnover in excess of £1m. But despite the scepticism towards him from some quarters, there was no doubt he had put in unstinting service over the years and Molloy commented: "I am full of admiration for the work he has done because he has had a tough time of it over a difficult period".

Supporters club treasurer, Mansell, agreed to take on the role after a handover period but he was to have a change of heart when he was made aware of just how much of a mess the accounting procedures were in. Mitchell had the dubious task of taking over as best he could.

Lippiatt was again in action on the signing-on front, this time giving youngsters Phil Ruggles, Simon Teague and Caleb Kamara-Taylor short-term deals. He then replaced assistant Dave Vaughan, who officially left because of work commitments, with Kevan Brown taking over, and, after a home postponement against Kettering Town, The Cards bounced back from their Cumbrian catastrophe with a 3-3 draw at Chester City in a cracker of a match. But the league form was still far from convincing – a 3-0 win at Kingstonian on New Year's Day the first triumph in seven Conference outings.

It took until 10 February before the next win arrived against Dover Athletic – by which time Woking had signed a player on loan who would become the catalyst for avoiding relegation. Chris Sharpling had played around 8 times for Crystal Palace in the Nationwide First Division. His arrival, in a 0-0 draw at Boston, came after a 2-1 FA Trophy defeat at home to Margate – a match that saw the last involvement of Wye, who was unhappy with losing his place in the team. Sharpling's first goal came a week later at Nuneaton Borough before he stunned the Kingfield crowd with a wonder goal in the 4-1 home triumph against Dover Athletic. In all he hit nine goals in 14 appearances – his double at Stevenage in a 3-0 win a highlight.

The rest of the season was played out without too much incident. Skipper West was called up by John Owens for the England semi-professional side, a selection that

Charlie Griffin takes aim against The Daggers.

appeared to be long overdue, and The Cards finished a respectable fourteenth in the table, with Lippiatt having been given the board's backing with an extension on his contract to the summer of 2003.

There was talk of the club moving into the full-time arena for the following season, Lippiatt having presented a blueprint for the club's future encompassing youth, finances, coaching, dieticians – in fact you name it, it was included. But he might as well not have bothered. Like McGovern and McDermott before him, Lippiatt was not destined to last the distance as manager and the club were about as far away from moving full-time as they had ever been.

10

Enter the Mystery Benefactor
2001/02

Hindsight would reveal that those who dared to predict this would be a season of stability and that further upheaval would be pushed aside, were optimistic in the extreme. It was to be a period when the constitution of Woking Football Club would be changed forever, with the revolutionary steps taken to allow one man overall power at Kingfield. Without that rule change in the memorandum and articles of association, Woking Football Club would have seen the season out in the hands of administrators rather than looking at a promising future with a multi-millionaire at the helm.

On the playing side, yet another manager failed to last the season out while the return of the most successful boss in the club's history didn't stop The Cards coming as close to relegation as it is possible to do without the trap door actually opening for them. When the dust finally settled at the end of another traumatic term in the Conference, there was much to reflect upon. Dwelling on just how calamitous the season could have been on all fronts, had the circumstances been different, was enough to form a bead of sweat upon many a furrowed brow.

Before a ball of the new season had been kicked, the club's AGM finally took place in the close season after delays regarding the completion of accounts. Two directors of vast experience stood down from their positions. Bill Sutton had already announced his intention to vacate and his leaving was no surprise. Likewise Paul Elmer, property director and a man who had first worked at Woking as a gateman in 1957. He had decided he'd had enough a few months before and was now officially relinquishing his role as a director. "I have become more and more frustrated at the lack of progress we are making and the fact that we are not achieving," Elmer had said. "It's only a personal view but I think we could have done more as a club in the last few years. We don't seem to have an overall plan we can work towards. It's all ifs and buts."

For a man who had put in six days a week at the club, he was able to speak with authority. "He was one of the three or four people who ran this club during the week and the others don't realise how much they'll miss him," said one Kingfield insider. Elmer had given invaluable advice while the sale of the freehold land occupied by the Chris Lane Health and Leisure Club had gone through at the height of the financial troubles. That sale of the so-called 'crown jewels' eventually earned the club around £350,000. And he was also on hand to help with negotiations for a ground share agreement with Brentford, with the Londoners granted an option to use Kingfield from the 2002/03 season if they so wished. Woking were paid a retainer for a situation which never came to fruition.

Loan star Geoff Pitcher in typically energetic form at Kingfield, this time against Forest Green Rovers.

Taking the place of Elmer and Sutton were John Dukes, as commercial director, and Bob Daborn as administration director. Ground and safety officer Mike Bidmead had stood for election to the board but, after missing out in the voting, had been co-opted onto the board as company secretary. Phil Shorter, having left his position on the commercial team in 1997 after becoming disillusioned with the club's lack of ambition, returned as commercial manager saying he had "unfinished business". He went on:

There has been limited communication in the past but we are nothing without our supporters and they can play their part. The club nearly did not exist because there was no cohesive strategy to move forward. There was no robust business plan and as soon as the success on the pitch waned it affected the off-the-pitch performance which in turn reduced our ability to compete. We aim to change that.

A new corporate initiative named Team Woking was introduced as Woking became a brand name. "We are looking to develop a range of products whereby fans can approach us and buy them via the club", enthused Dukes. "It is my aim that we get to a point where we don't have to rely on gate receipts." In reality the situation had become too severe for a solution to be found easily, although the new initiatives sparked by John Buchanan, Peter Jordan, Dukes and Shorter certainly had short-term impact.

Colin Lippiatt, who had become the fourth full-time manager at Kingfield in as many years when he signed a three-year deal in the close season, was once again optimistic for the new season. Scott Steele had agreed a player/coaching role, with Kevan Brown

Charlie Griffin takes on the Forest Green Rovers defence.

stepping up to become assistant manager. It was again a summer of activity as far as Lippiatt was concerned. Scott Huckerby and Warren Haughton were brought in to boost the attacking options, the former with Conference experience at Telford United, the latter purely on a recommendation. Haughton was moving south and was looking for a club. Hampton and Richmond were said to have offered around £200-a-week to the striker but Lippiatt stepped in with an offer double that – with the result that he got his man. A player who had never played in non-League's top division was suddenly a Card.

Haughton brought with him a proven goal-scoring record with Doc Martens Premier side Tamworth and Lippiatt, who admitted he had never seen Haughton play, accepted it was a gamble. "It was all down to a tip off," said the boss;

Some of the prices I have been quoted for players has meant it has not been possible to get them in. There is always an element of doubt when someone hasn't played at Conference level but when you look at Warren's CV in black and white there is no getting away from the fact that in three years, he has scored a lot of goals.

Haughton managed to find the net just twice in the Conference during the season, while another Warren – Patmore – had opted for full-time football with Rushden & Diamonds rather than rejoin his old Yeovil boss at Kingfield. The old saying you get what you pay for was appropriate in this case. Paul Steele and Dave Piper were the other early summer recruits, but few would have envisaged the massive row which erupted at Kingfield prior to the big kick-off at Chester City.

Barry Moore whips in a cross against Doncaster Rovers.

It centred on three players, all midfielders. Matt Hayfield, Steve Perkins and Nick Roddis were all chosen to represent the British Universities at the World Student Games in China. Their inclusion in the touring party was a real honour for the trio – but would mean Lippiatt's plans being totally disrupted as they would miss the first five league matches of the season. The boss made his feelings known in no uncertain terms, firstly to Hayfield, who had written to Lippiatt even before the travelling party had been confirmed saying that he intended to go if selected. At that stage Perkins indicated he was "95 per cent sure of staying", while Roddis' selection had not even been mooted in the early stages of the dispute. In the event, all three were destined to go to China and Lippiatt fumed:

It's not about personalities it's about the principle. I'm pleased they have been selected but in my opinion they should have made the decision in five minutes flat that they were going to stay. I expect players to show loyalty no matter who they are. The tournament has been badly timed. If it had been in the summer there would be no problem. If it had been the England semi-pro side I would be obliged to release them. But in this case I could do something about it and that's what I've done.

That something was to suggest to Hayfield that he stay away from Kingfield for two weeks pending the selection. "If he's going there's no point in him being here and if he goes to China he knows he won't ever play for Woking again," said Lippiatt. Hayfield never played for Woking again.

The case with Roddis and Perkins was less straightforward. Hayfield's form had waned and there was talk of him not being the player he was when he first arrived at the club. He was certainly not indispensable. Perkins and Roddis were very much part of Lippiatt's plans and when it was rubber-stamped that they would be joining Hayfield on the trip, Lippiatt was again quick to react. He threatened to leave the club if the directors failed to back him in his desire to cite the players for breach of contract. And Lippiatt was angry that Perkins had "categorically told me he was staying" and then had "tried to manipulate a better deal" before the midfielder was alleged to have left a message on the boss' mobile phone saying, 'I've decided to go to China, cheers Steve Perkins".

The row continued for weeks with Lippiatt having said that the pair "should never play for Woking again and I'll be amazed if the directors disagree with me". The directors did not disagree. However, both players would play for the club again, Lippiatt would stay and the club back down from their rigid stance. The problem that arose from the whole mess was that Lippiatt had gone ahead and signed Barry Moore, Terry McFlynn, Michael Fowler and Gareth Graham as midfield replacements. With 'keeper Tony Tucker, Paul Steele, Huckerby, Haughton, and Dave Piper already snapped up there was suddenly an abundance of players. Tucker replaced Vince Matassa, who had broken his hand in a freak accident at home. The Australian was destined never to wear The Cards' number one jersey again as by the time he was fit he was on his way back to his homeland and a new club, Perth Glory.

After Scott Steele had enjoyed a bumper testimonial against Spurs at Kingfield, the season got underway at last, in Cheshire.

Minus Perkins, Roddis and Hayfield, but with a smattering of the new recruits, Woking could not have asked for a better start. Having managed to cross the picket line of Chester supporters – protesting about chairman Terry Smith's handling of the club – Haughton scored after 51 seconds and Moore added a second in a 2-0 victory. It proved a false dawn. The next four matches against Boston United, Morecambe, Dagenham & Redbridge and Scarborough brought a return of precisely no points and the doom merchants were once again forecasting a winter of discontent.

The respite from those defeats came where many would least have expected it. Huish Park in Yeovil is never the easiest place to go and get a result. Dean Chandler, who was hovering in the background and had signed the week before knowing he could not be paid, got his chance, and he and Junior Kadi, who Lippiatt had known from his Kingstonian days, were suddenly thrust into the team. Both men did not let their boss down in a 3-1 win which dumbfounded the critics. Huckerby lobbed a superb first, then turned provider by playing a one-two with his strike partner Charlie Griffin who raced clear and slotted a second. Carl Alford gave the home side hope with a goal a minute before the break, before Woking were subjected to a second-half barrage. Not only did they survive, they then had the audacity to score a third when Kadi raced half the length of the pitch to poke the ball past 'keeper Jon Sheffield. "That performance stands out, not in terms of quality, but in pride and resilience and wanting to wear the Woking shirt," enthused Lippiatt afterwards.

Once again there was a modicum of upheaval on the commercial side with Shorter resigning just weeks into his job as commercial manager for personal reasons. Scott

Roscoe D'Sane scores a cracker against Donny.

Steele was relieved of his coaching duties just a month into the season for no apparent reason other than Lippiatt having another change of heart.

Despite all the protestations to the contrary, the next fixture at Doncaster Rovers saw the return of Roddis to the starting line-up and Perkins to the substitutes bench. Both had been sacked but won their appeals and the duo were adamant about putting the whole saga behind them. "People should remember that Nick and Steve were never going to be allowed to leave this club without us getting a fee," said Lippiatt. "I was without five players so I decided that they should be brought back in. It's time to get back to football matters."

As if the script had been written, Roddis scored Woking's only goal in a 1-1 draw, his effort coming direct from a corner. "I've been practising that in China," quipped the 31-year-old after the final whistle. The irony was that, now that Lippiatt had welcomed his two dissenters back into the fold, he had eight midfield players on the books. The reserve side having been scrapped at the end of the previous season merely exacerbated the problem. "The likelihood is that one or two will have to go," admitted the boss.

The atrocities in New York on Tuesday 11 September made the home match against Margate that evening pretty meaningless. Many could not believe that football was carrying on in such circumstances and what proved to be Woking's lowest crowd of the season, just 1,216, created an eerie atmosphere on a night where the game seemed irrelevant. A 1-0 defeat meant that The Cards had picked up just 7 points from their opening 8 matches. Few Woking fans expected the next development in what had already become another eventful season despite it being in its infancy.

Having tracked his progress over the past few months, Woking had put in a bid to Crystal Palace of £60,000 for Chris Sharpling, who had enjoyed such a productive loan spell the previous season. The surprise was not in the fact that the bid had been accepted, but more to do with how a club, still haemorrhaging money as far as trading was concerned, could suddenly afford to splash out that sort of money for a player? Speculating to accumulate is the nature of the game in the football business. But asking people to accept that sort of dramatic turnaround without asking the question, particularly with the attendance being at an all-time low for the club in the Conference, was never going to happen. The answer would come in the new year with the arrival of a so-called mystery benefactor.

Cue surprise number two. The fans were by now expecting a new striker. What they did not expect was someone other than Sharpling putting pen to paper. The man The Cards had suddenly turned to was England semi-professional legend Patmore, who had come close to joining in the summer before he opted for the Football League and Rushden & Diamonds instead. But Patmore had become disillusioned with the full-time game and revealed that he was "bored after two months and hating football". Having phoned Lippiatt to ask whether he was still interested in signing him, his former Yeovil boss jumped at the chance. The transfer fee of £42,500 was duly handed over to Rushden boss Brian Talbot who was agreeable to let an unhappy player move on – provided his club got the signing on fee that they had shelled out. The amount of the fee reflected exactly that sum. "When a player of his quality becomes available we have to be interested," said vice chairman John Buchanan. "Although Stevenage wanted him, he wanted to re-sign for Colin and we're delighted," added a man who was doing his utmost to help Lippiatt behind the scenes.

More Donny action, this time it's David Piper bending a leg.

Meanwhile, the bid for Sharpling still stood but, in contrast to Patmore, he wanted to stay in the Football League. Had Sharpling already made the decision to sign, it is unlikely the funds would have been made available for Patmore – but the directors took a gamble and went for one, just in case the move for the other did not come off. Then there were two, as the saying goes.

Patmore's arrival sparked a flurry of excitement among supporters. After all, here was a big name, still only 30, who had committed himself to a life at Kingfield until May 2004. Two weeks earlier, Doncaster Rovers had paid £150,000 for a certain Justin Jackson. On that basis there was no denying that the Patmore deal was a snip. He had become the seventh ex-Yeovil player to sign for the club in two years and brought the international contingent up to five at that time.

He promptly scored on his debut in a 3-1 victory at home to Northwich Victoria. Steve West and substitute McFlynn were the others on target. Unfortunately, the game will also be remembered for the dreadful knee injury suffered by Paul Steele which kept him out of first team action for fifteen months. Patmore's second strike came four days later at Forest Green Rovers. But by the time he notched from close range, The Cards were down to nine men having had Roddis and Moore sent off. A further four other Woking players were booked in the 2-1 defeat, although the locals must have wondered whether they had stumbled on a Woking training session before kick-off with more than twenty players in Cards' colours warming up. It summed up just how overburdened with personnel the squad had become. Lippiatt needed to take action and he placed three men on the transfer list. Scott Steele was the shock name, while Martin Randall and Fowler joined him. Graham's month-to-month contract was not renewed.

If Woking had an abundance of midfield players they were soon to have a glut of strikers too when Sharpling finally signed in a £60,000 move. The rumours were that Crystal Palace would have released him in a month or two anyway and The Cards could have had him for nothing. No matter, Woking were suddenly a spending club, having shelled out £132,500 since the summer. They had transformed from a club that sold their best player for £20,000 to pay wages two years earlier, to one of the Conference big spenders. This despite being weighed down by a greater playing budget and an average crowd of 600 less than the breakeven figure. The money was obviously coming from somewhere. The £150,000 received from Woking Council, as the second tranche of monies from the sale of land occupied by Chris Lane, was a help, but not necessarily used for player purchase. In fact many believed the council money merely acted as a smokescreen.

With a £100,000 strike partnership on the books, suddenly Woking had become a potent force in attack and a 4-0 triumph at home over Dover Athletic saw Patmore grab a brace. However, despite his goal heroics the previous season, it would take Sharpling 13 matches to get off the mark – incredible given his record while a loan player. A passionate display in a 1-1 draw with Stevenage Borough, with Griffin earning the plaudits as a replacement 'keeper when Tucker went off with concussion, did little to improve the league position and there was no doubt that Lippiatt was beginning to feel the strain. From a manager with little budget he had suddenly spent a small fortune in

Dominic Reece fires over a cross against The Railwaymen of Leigh RMI.

Conference terms and was being judged accordingly. The directors who had backed him now wanted results.

Away defeats at Hayes and Leigh RMI were followed by a home tie against Newport County in the fourth qualifying round of the FA Cup. With prize money of £20,000 up for grabs it was a chance for Woking to get some of their money back, but County boss Tim Harris taunted The Cards. "Let's see if they've got any bottle," was one jibe before the tie. "I can't see how they need £20,000 after spending more than £100,000 on two players," was another.

A 0-0 draw at Kingfield, with Patmore missing a sitter which would have taken them through to a first-round clash at Blackpool, meant a replay in South Wales. Two years earlier it had been Burton Albion. Then was the turn of Carlisle United. Now came a new low for the club in the FA's premier competition. A dismal 3-1 defeat at another Doc Martens side who piled on the pressure until their prey gave up without so much as a whimper. That Newport result and performance was the last straw for Lippiatt who, sensing the writing was on the wall, engineered the homecoming of an old friend of both the club and himself. He needed help to improve morale – and results.

Geoff Chapple strode through the gates at Kingfield as though he had never been away and Lippiatt admitted:

The pressure has been lifted off my shoulders and it's more of a relief than anything. I didn't want to leave Woking and what has happened is in the best interests of the club. I can just get on now with what I love doing and that's to coach.

Chapple was excited and he commented:

I'm ecstatic to be back and I'm still terribly ambitious. I never achieved Football League status here before and that's the aim although there is a lot of work to do. I never wanted to leave in the first place and only did so because the club couldn't offer me the security of a contract.

Unfortunately for Chapple, he was destined to leave much sooner than he thought. For the time being though, it was as if the great man had never been away and while there was a division among supporters as to whether reinstating him was a wise move, the deal was done. Those against the decision thought the club had taken a backward step and argued it was impossible to turn back the clock. Those in favour were hoping Chapple could roll back the years and rescue The Cards from five years of decline. The man himself ignored the old saying you should never go back and he had Terry Molloy's endorsement ringing in his ears. "This is the opportunity for Woking to become the force we once were", enthused the chairman.

One man's gain is always another man's loss and in the management reshuffle, Brown suffered the indignity of being told by Lippiatt via a phonecall that his services were no longer required. There was no doubt that Brown's departure was dealt with

Barry Moore fires home against Leigh.

shabbily and was a sad end to his second spell at Woking. His wages were used in the restructure, with Lippiatt taking a cut and Chapple being accommodated within the existing budget.

Chapple's first match in charge on his return was at home to Hereford United on Saturday 3 November 2001. Scott Steele, placed on the transfer list by Lippiatt after being told he was not part of his plans, returned to his favourite position behind the front two now that Chapple was picking the team and he produced a wonderful display. His goal gave Chapple three points on his return in a 1-0 win.

With Ralph Ellis another important signing as commercial manager – The Cards beat off the likes of Bolton Wanderers and Portsmouth for his signature – there was an expectant air at Kingfield. Chapple had one remit when he took over – to reduce the playing staff and with it the wage bill. It was no mean task. "I haven't come in to wield the axe but the squad is too big, especially with no reserve side," he said after inheriting twenty-six players. Rumours of a £60,000 bid from Stevenage for Patmore were quashed by Chapple, who said his centre forward was going nowhere.

Griffin was the first to go after becoming unsettled because of limited opportunities. Havant & Waterlooville on loan was his port of call but, ironically, he would return and score some vital goals in a Woking shirt towards the end of the season. Chandler, not on contract, was also surplus to requirements and was another to go. While Chapple was desperate to offload, he had the problem of dealing with players he did not want who were on two-year deals. If they did not want to go, they only had to tow the line to stay and pick up their money.

In the meantime, Chapple brought in Brian McGorry and Lloyd Webber, who didn't stay, and Roscoe D'Sane and Dominic Reece who did. Another recruit was former Card Eddie Saunders and later on goalkeeper Scott Bevan arrived on loan from Southampton to replace the inexperienced Tucker. The most significant signing of all was midfielder Geoff Pitcher, who was on loan for three months from Brighton. As it turned out Pitcher was instrumental in The Cards staying in the Conference. But it was in the boardroom where the real action was about to happen.

There had been speculation for around a year that a loyal fan was prepared to pump money into the ailing club to help preserve its future. That time was about to come. In December, 79 shareholders indicated their overwhelming support for Chris Ingram ahead of an extraordinary general meeting on 12 February. The reason for their faith in Ingram was because there was no other way out of trouble. Debts of around £200,000 a year could not be sustained indefinitely and the financial facts were laid bare at the meeting. The choice was simple. Allow Ingram a majority shareholding or go bust.

Up until now it had been a members club with one share, one vote. For the sake of saving Woking Football Club a change of constitution to allow one man overall control needed to be sanctioned. Here was an individual who was not only a long-standing fan of the club but he just happened to have a reported £70m to his name after selling his media space and advertising company. Suddenly the purchase of Patmore and

Geoff Pitcher sets his sights on goal against the Hilton Park outfit.

Sharpling, and the appointment of a new commercial manager (Ellis), not to mention a stadium manager, Peter Winter, made more sense.

As well as the impending cash injection in exchange for shares, a major sponsorship deal with telepeople.com – signed up by Ellis and Dukes – was said to be potentially one of the most lucrative in the Conference. Things were looking up except that, despite Chapple's arrival, results on the pitch remained mixed with wins against Chester and Farnborough but defeats to Barnet, Boston United, Morecambe and Scarborough.

FA Trophy success against Welling United and Kingstonian were made meaning-less by a 3-0 home trouncing by Burton Albion. Similarly, a Steve Perkins-inspired 4-1 league win at Stevenage was sweet but meant The Cards were barely doing enough to keep pace with those fighting the dreaded drop. The situation was not helped by the loss of Jamie Pitman, who decided to have an operation to remove a bone growing on the back of his foot. The good news was that Pitcher's influence was beginning to show.

22 January 2002 was a red-letter day when Lippiatt was sacked as head coach in acrimonious circumstances. "I think they felt that my face was still around and things haven't changed so they have switched the blame onto me," he said after receiving a phonecall from director John Buchanan;

It seems that one minute I'm the hero and the next I'm being told 'all the best but we've finished with you.' I agreed to shift to one side to allow Geoff to come back and

I lost a lot of money on my contract because I took a reduction. It's no secret they've got to pay me six months' money but that's a lot less than it would have been on my original contract.

Lippiatt was unhappy that Chapple did not make a case for him to stay. For his part, Chapple was adamant he could not see the move to sack Lippiatt coming. "We've been together for so many years and it's a shock. To be honest it's like a bereavement," said Chapple. While some saw Lippiatt's departure as sad in view of the fact that he had done so much for Woking, others viewed his departure as inevitable if the club was going to move on. As for Chapple, he wasted no time in asking former Southampton midfielder Glenn Cockerill to fill the coaching role on a temporary basis – an appointment which was to become a permanent one. The 43-year-old more than made up for his lack of knowledge of the non-League game with his positive mental attitude and his desire to instil some of the battling qualities he possessed as a player into the Woking squad.

Between them, Chapple and Cockerill managed an escape route from the bottom three – just. A dramatic win at Stalybridge Celtic, with goals from Griffin and Roscoe D'Sane, could not have been more crucial. Once again it had been one long struggle to survive among non-League's elite, except this time it had been mighty close.

But there was a silver lining – because for the first time in years, The Cards could at least look forward to a financially secure future.

There's been a Goal at Nuneaton
2002/03

For a variety of reasons, some seasons come and go without so much as a backward glance. They might blend into the blur of mediocrity, or lack the kind of incidents which stir the memory in subsequent years. Sometimes, it is simply because they were so bad they are quickly erased from the mind, either consciously or otherwise.

Ask any of the Woking contingent among the 3,049 fans at Kingfield on 26 April whether they remember season 2002/03 and the answer would be a deafening "yes" – as loud as the roar which greeted the final whistle on that never-to-be-forgotten afternoon when Telford United were beaten 3-0 on the final day of the season.

Rare statistics, strange sequences, an inordinate number of players used, drama and near catastrophe do not begin to explain an incredible nine months. Not by a long chalk. Except this time, most of the events – good, bad or indifferent – happened on the pitch. Mostly they were bad in a period of serious underachievement. But the season had started with a bang and a brief time at the top of the league. Then, inevitably some would say, reality set in. The campaign ended with a game of Russian roulette to decide who would take the plunge into the Ryman League. The Gods were with The Cards and they stayed up, but only those who were among that last day throng could tell you just how close it had been.

Relegation is a harmless enough word in isolation but its meaning has serious ramifications. For the past few years, it had reared its ugly head from time to time at Kingfield, but it had maintained a respectful distance and never felt the need to engage the club in head-to-head conflict. That was until the culmination of a roller-coaster season which really will live long in the memory – although certainly not for the quality of the football.

There was little indication during the previous season of the drama to come. No sooner had 2001/02 ended than Geoff Chapple went to work on reducing his bulging squad. He had managed to avoid the drop the previous season thanks mainly to the players he had brought in – notably Geoff Pitcher – but the midfielder, along with Eddie Saunders, Roscoe D'Sane, Dominic Reece, Jamie Pitman, Steve Perkins, Charlie Griffin and Warren Haughton were to go their separate ways for a variety of reasons.

With the collapse of ITV Digital there were suddenly a flood of discarded players on the available list as Nationwide League clubs tightened their belts and were in no position to renew contracts to fringe players. And because there were so many ex-League personnel on the market, there was a swing in power towards the clubs – with players desperate to get a contract wherever they could. "We must get the right ones in", said Chapple:

With Mr Ingram's professional approach we will be running a tight ship and the days of signing on fees and big wages are long gone. Some of them will get a bit of a shock when they come through my door and I tell them what's on offer. I want people to come to Woking not for me, Glenn Cockerill (coach) or money but because they are passionate about the club.

Nice sentiments but the reality was that Woking might as well have been Welling, Worcester, Worksop or Worthing as far as players were concerned. They were passionate about getting a job never mind the name of the club. Some had never even visited Kingfield before, let alone worked up any sort of enthusiasm or affinity with the place.

Nevertheless, Chapple made it clear he would be choosy but feared that those he wanted to bring in would have to be turned away because of their demands. The club played the waiting game with the theory that delaying a signing would mean the player was likely to accept a lesser offer – or risk not getting a club. This made a mockery of Chapple's stance of bringing in only those passionate about Woking. In reality, it was a case of take what you can afford.

Behind the scenes, the club announced a long-term youth development scheme with a tie up with Woking College. The academy, as it would be known, provided a

Crowd favourite Nicky Banger on the attack against Leigh RMI.

The KRE up the noise level at Kingfield.

direct link for talented players between the age of between sixteen and nineteen, to the club's two senior sides – the reserves being reintroduced. "It will take time before we see the benefit, but boys will be given the chance to carry on their education while taking a football course," said Chapple. "We need a much more local theme at the football club and if we get one player through every two years I'll be happy."

Another unprecedented move at Kingfield was to appoint a full-time managing director who would double up as commercial manager/director. That man was Brian Blower, who replaced John Dukes and Ralph Ellis. Many felt Ellis was unlucky. He was a man with a wealth of football knowledge and he looked the part, but he did not fit into the new chairman's plans. Ingram was delighted to get his man, who was among a shortlist of five. Before the announcement at the club's annual meeting the chairman had said:

It's been important to get the right blend when choosing the candidate because it's an important role. As well as commercial and marketing responsibilities we need someone there to deal with the day-to-day running of the club so that I can have a less hands-on approach.

Shareholders were informed of Blower's appointment at the meeting while, as expected, John Buchanan and Phil Ledger retained their places on the board following

Glenn Cockerill takes temporary charge of the team and starts with a 1-0 win against high-flyers Chester City, managed by former Southampton team-mate, Mark Wright.

Ingram's recommendation for continuity. Blower's first priority was to find a main sponsor. "I can bring the expertise of commercial management to the role," he said. "I'm not being disrespectful but I don't think that Woking Football Club have really explored the full potential of the area. I'm not saying I'm going to do that on my own. I can only do that with the help of the staff and people that are already here."

Blower talked a good game but was soon under fire from supporters for being unable to attract a main sponsor, while in his first few months some key members of staff and the volunteers he was so keen to work with decided for varying reasons to leave. As first impressions go, his was not the most telling. But in fairness the way events unfolded on the pitch was enough to put any company off an association with the club. Ultimately, however, he did nothing but cause unrest and having failed in his job to attract sponsorship, he was sacked in the final weeks of the season after a fracas with ground and safety officer Mike Bidmead, who was also shown the door.

Chris Collins became the first new signing at Kingfield, joining from Doc Martens side Newport IOW for a nominal fee of around £5,000. Then it all went quiet on the recruitment front. Prior to the pre-season campaign, Chapple revealed: "I've seen about a dozen players in the past week but they are asking for signing on fees and big wages. It's all to do with economics. I'm not going to rush into anything."

Former favourite Grant Payne, whose cut-price sale to Aldershot Town in November 1999 had caused such a storm, was among forty 'trialists' hopeful of persuading Chapple they were worth a contract. His four-goal performance at Boreham Wood in a pre-season friendly helped towards a deal being agreed. Former Southampton forward Nicky Banger, ex-Sheffield United captain Lee Sandford, Rob Kember, Steve Farrelly,

Anthony Allman, Ben Abbey and ex-Rushden star Jon Brady joined him as new recruits. Brady's signing had not been straightforward and Chapple nearly went as far as pulling out of the deal when he discovered that the midfielder was playing Woking off against Chester City. Eventually Brady put pen to paper, but it was more a marriage of convenience than anything else and it would not be long before the association ended in acrimonious divorce.

With the late influx of players in place, Woking embarked on a Conference season given extra spice by the introduction of promotion play-offs. But given the scares at the other end of the table in recent years, promotion via the back door or any other route was not at the forefront of anyone's minds at Kingfield.

A 1-0 opening-day victory against Forest Green Rovers – in a new-look red kit – was the perfect start. While not convincing by any stretch of the imagination it represented Woking's first opening-day win at home in their Conference history – and only their third overall. Seven new faces made their Cards debuts and not since the first year in the top flight (1992/93) had there been such wholesale change. Just as he had done in the first match, Abbey scored his second goal four days later in a 1-1 draw at Nuneaton Borough.

By the time Chapple's men had produced back-to-back 3-0 triumphs against Kettering Town and Leigh RMI the unthinkable had happened. Woking were top of the Conference. There was a disbelieving air of euphoria around Kingfield and not only were the team winning, they were playing some scintillating football in patches thanks to Brady and Banger operating as good old-fashioned wingers. "We're playing with a bit

Jamie Campbell, a new recruit from Stevenage, impresses for The Cards.

of style and the aim is to get the ball wide and get crosses in," said Chapple, who was keen to play down the club's elevated position. The sceptics, who pointed to the fact that the opposition in the first four matches were bound to be relegation candidates come the end of the season, had every reason to be cautious.

"We haven't played the likes of Doncaster, Chester and Yeovil yet and it's the oldest cliché in the book but we have to take one match at a time," added the boss, who was delighted with 10 points from 4 matches. "We're bound to have a rocky ride at some stage so it's great to get some points in the bag early on."

Nobody could have envisaged what happened next. As if just 3 points from the next 11 matches was bad enough, conceding 36 goals in the process was embarrassing in the extreme. As a fall from grace it could not have been more dramatic and by the next time Woking picked up three points for a win, Chapple had been given his marching orders. That seemed inconceivable as The Cards travelled to Scarborough for the fifth match of the campaign and earned a 1-1 draw. Only a last-minute equaliser cancelled out Brady's first goal for the club – and prevented Chapple from picking up the manager of the month award.

Chapple made a public plea for help in keeping Sandford at Kingfield as his budget was stretched. He was mightily impressed with the central defender and added that Jon Boardman alongside him reminded him of Rio Ferdinand. In the coming weeks, both men began defending like Les Ferdinand never mind Rio. But for the time being, Sandford was accommodated.

A crowd of 2,721 turned up on a Tuesday night for the home match against Gravesend & Northfleet. They were to witness Woking's first defeat of the season as the cracks in the defence began to surface. A home defeat by Hereford United, again by the odd goal, was more water polo than football but the match went the duration mainly because Sky TV cameras were in attendance. A third successive reverse at home, this time to Northwich Victoria, was witnessed by 1,072 fewer people than the Gravesend clash and crowds would get lower before 'Black September' was out. Margate, Morecambe, Yeovil Town – again on Sky – and Stevenage Borough followed. An horrendous 19 goals were conceded in those four matches while The Cards found the net just twice.

Goalkeeper Steve Farrelly had been replaced after the Yeovil clash but understudy Tony Tucker could do no better in what had been the ultimate humiliation – a 5-1 defeat at home to fierce rivals Stevenage. The club had gone from top of the league at the end of August to third from bottom a month later. The slide down the table could not have been more startling. Still Chapple and coach Cockerill kept their jobs and Ingram backed both but added: "Now is time for action. I have given Geoff and Glenn a brief and it's down to them to come to me with an action plan. Enough is enough and we can't have more of the same."

Courtesy of Tottenham Hotspur, Shwan Jalal became the third goalkeeper of the campaign as a 2-2 draw against Burton Albion stopped the rot and helped avert the worst run of defeats for twenty-seven years. It still ranks as the fourth worst run of results in The Cards' 114-year history – probably the worst if you consider that 27 goals had been conceded in 7 games.

'What's going on?' – Glenn Cockerill in animated mood.

A wonder goal from Barry Moore stunned everyone in the ground at Victoria Road in a midweek match four days later as Woking went in front against Dagenham & Redbridge within two minutes of the kick-off. Former Cards Steve West and Steve Perkins were largely anonymous for the home side but The Daggers struck back and a great goal from Mark Janney, engineered by Mark Stein, gave the hosts a point which in truth they deserved. The trip to Southport on Saturday 12 October 2002 was another one of those dates of historical interest. It proved to be Chapple's last match in charge of his beloved Woking.

After the encouragement of two draws, a dreadful 5-1 defeat – in which coach Glenn Cockerill played – was the last straw for Chris Ingram and his directors. The chairman was quick to take action and summoned Chapple to a meeting at Kingfield at 9 a.m. on the Monday morning. While Chapple's departure was engineered as a resignation to make it look better for all parties, the simple truth was that the man who had tried and failed to revive the glory days was sacked.

"It's very sad because Geoff is an essential part of the history of this club," said Ingram:

Personally, some of the happiest days of my life have been spent following the exploits of Woking Football Club under the guidance of Geoff. But I've been under pressure to do something which I've ignored and the writing has been on the wall. I would love for it to have worked out with Geoff and I hope that he lands on his feet because he deserves that. But the club is bigger than any one person.

The irony was that once again a Woking manager had lost his job following a debacle at Haig Avenue, Brian McDermott having already suffered that fate in February 2000.

What surprised many fans was that Cockerill, as his number two, was not ousted along with the manager. After all, hadn't he been part of where it had all gone wrong? But Ingram had seen enough in Cockerill to hand him the role of caretaker boss, if only to give him a chance while he considered the long-term position. The outcome was that the 43-year-old former Southampton midfielder was given four matches to prove himself starting with a home clash against Chester City.

By this time Sean Evers and Wayne Burnett had been brought in before disappearing without a trace, while Brady had become disillusioned with the results and lined up a move to Chester after all – but not before causing unrest in the dressing room. He was reportedly the influence behind skipper Moore making demands of the club for bonus money – cash being his main motivation it seemed – and his leaving the club brought some much-needed harmony among the players.

Sandford, who had endured a shocking time on the pitch of late, was soon discarded while Ian Simpemba had arrived on loan from Wycombe Wanderers. So Cockerill was now in charge and he wasted no time in stamping his own mark on the team by bringing in former Fulham and Reading midfielder Neil Smith from Stevenage and Ian Hamilton from Lincoln City. Both had worked with Cockerill before.

Nobody really expected The Cards to beat Chester, managed by Mark Wright, a former team-mate of Cockerill at Southampton, on 19 October, but an 84th-minute penalty from Abbey gave the new man in charge the perfect start with a 1-0 win. It was a year after Chapple had resumed his Kingfield career with the same winning score against Hereford.

Cockerill, with three matches to come against Luton Town in the LDV Vans Trophy, Dover in the FA Cup and Telford United in the Conference, made it known he wanted the job permanently. The 2-0 reverse against Luton hardly mattered but the cup tie at The Crabble was vital in financial terms. With the club still haemorrhaging money, a cup run would help. A man called Nicky Dent almost did that to Woking's hopes of making the first round there and then when he put Dover in front, but Simpemba's equaliser gave The Cards a 1-1 draw. The same player had a glorious chance to seal it in the 85th-minute, but he shot straight at 'keeper Paul Hyde from six yards. Ultimately it proved costly as a disastrous 2-1 defeat in the replay at Kingfield saw The Cards once again blow up against Doc Martens League opposition.

So Cockerill went into his fifth match in charge – the cup replay obviously not in the scheduled four – away at Telford and a 1-0 defeat in driving rain, with only 743 people watching, saw his team plunge into the bottom two. One win, one draw and three defeats was his record but the professionalism, work-rate and attitude instilled in the players, with Neil Smith and Hamilton bringing much-needed resolve to the team, held considerable sway with Ingram.

"There are four options open to us", said the chairman:

The first is to say to Glenn, sorry but that's it, we don't want you. The second is to look for a new manager and ask Glenn to put his hat in the ring with other applicants. Thirdly, we could give him until the end of the year to improve results, or we could confirm his position until the end of the season.

The fourth option was favoured and Cockerill was appointed – with the carrot of a two-year deal proposed if Woking stayed in the Conference. "I had a gut feeling I'd be offered the job and now I have I'll make sure I get this club back to where it belongs," said a delighted Cockerill:

I have been given until the end of the season with a review in April and I fully understand that because I'm inexperienced at this level of management. But it's a great opportunity for me and I'm delighted that the chairman and the board have given me the chance to show what I can do.

The beginning of November represented the sad departure from the club of the last link with the glory days, as Scott Steele accepted a pay-off after being told he was not part of Cockerill's plans. The 31-year-old Scot had been a tremendously skilful and willing performer and had given Woking fans a decade of entertainment, wonderful goals and passion for the shirt.

Record signing Chris Sharpling takes up the challenge against Morecambe.

The Conference had moved on, however, and Cockerill felt he needed to up the fitness level of the team, which involved discarding a crowd favourite. With the subject of going full-time again talked about, and Cockerill declaring he ultimately only wanted players who could train during the day in the long-term, another influential player was to leave the club. Barry Moore had apparently told Cockerill that, "he only wanted to play for a laugh and was not interested in being a full-time professional footballer". From that moment his days were numbered.

The midfielder's agent wanted a pay-off for his man but Cockerill refused, saying only that he would cancel Moore's registration. The deed was done and Moore – the club's player of the year the previous season— ended up at Crawley Town before making a life for himself in the USA. The player news was coming thick and fast. Boardman was selected for the England semi-professional squad, while Jon Coates, from Swansea, and Raphael Nade, from Welling, both put pen to paper. Tucker went on loan to Walton.

Backroom staff Barry Kimber, the club's legendary physiotherapist, and Ron Rawlings, the kit man, were both recovering from illness – in Kimber's case a life-saving stomach operation. It meant he had to give up his physiotherapist role but he remained, along with Rawlings, as a valuable member of the matchday team.

The finances were mentioned once again in a press conference and the bleak prognosis just would not go away. The only difference now was that Ingram, a multi-millionaire, was in charge. Having made a trading loss of £165,000 in 1999, £160,000 in 2000 and £230,617 in 2001, it was announced that Woking FC Ltd (the trading arm of the club) lost a staggering £475,314 for the ten months to May 2002. The balance sheet deficit was now in excess of £1m. Shareholders funds of around £417,000 a year from the 835 shares issued at that time would not even cover the annual loss and anyway, with Ingram owning 751 of those shares – having recently increased his personal holding, the financial burden lay primarily at his door. "We're years away from breaking even", he admitted. "Just a small loss each year would be regarded as a success and with the shareholders' funds not covering the losses I'm afraid we're into old-fashioned patronage."

That statement alone spoke volumes for his commitment to ensuring the club would survive. He would put in around £1m before the season was out in addition to his annual outlay of around £400,000. Those fans thinking that Ingram could have done more with the playing budget were swiftly reminded by others that without this man at the helm there wouldn't be a club.

A change on the board saw Keith Owen, who had experience in the media as well as business knowledge, be appointed as a director as a replacement for Julian Goulding. David Seward, formerly secretary at Surrey and Somerset Cricket Clubs, was soon installed as company secretary in place of Bidmead.

Cockerill's early run of results as permanent boss had seen a 0-0 draw with Barnet, a 2-0 win at Burton Albion – under the viewing eyes of Brian Clough watching his son Nigel – and a 3-1 reverse at Doncaster in front of the TV cameras for the third time in the season.

Classy Scott Canham did much to keep Woking in the Conference.

The Burton and Doncaster results were the start of something incredible. Woking set what is believed to be a Conference record for their 11-match run, in which a win was followed by a loss. This sequence kept the club above the relegation places, which were filled by Kettering Town, Forest Green Rovers and Stevenage Borough in early December. Halifax, Northwich, Nuneaton, Kettering and Scarborough were the teams who succumbed to The Cards' new-found self belief but only one of those wins was away from home.

The worrying aspect about the defeats in between was that two of them were 5-0. Both were in quick succession at Hereford United and neighbours Farnborough, who were about to lose seven of their players to Stevenage in the unsavoury 'Graham Westley affair'. Farnborough became the sixth team to score five goals past The Cards and nobody could quite believe it after the steady improvement of recent weeks. Of the Hereford result, Cockerill had been moved to say: "It was a 5-0 but not like a 5-0 in September". What he probably meant was that, in his view, it had not been a capitulation and was down primarily to individual errors and his own desire to chase the game, leaving gaps in defence. But 5-0 was 5-0 in most fans' eyes and it could well have been more.

The other concern in the amazing run was that the defeats included matches against Forest Green, Leigh and Gravesend – all six-pointers at the time. Cockerill had insisted on playing a 4-3-3 formation in matches where he didn't want to lose, which seemed a strange tactic. Margate were another who would later win such a hugely important meeting.

There had been low points in September but there was an equally depressing spell in the space of a week at the end of January and into early February. The embarrassing 1-0 Surrey Senior Cup defeat at home to Dulwich Hamlet, of the Ryman Division One South, was inept and highlighted the quality, or lack of it, Cockerill had at the club. One of the lowest competitive crowds in the club's history, just 204, gave an indication of the importance of this much derided competition, but even so, it was not an excuse for such a horror show on the last Tuesday in January.

A week later, after a goalless draw at Gloucester City on the Saturday, Woking lost for the second time against a team two leagues below them. This time, however, it was in the FA Trophy. This time it mattered. The 2-0 reverse at home saw Cockerill brand his team "pathetic". He went on:

I feel as though the players have let down me, the fans and everybody associated with the club. It's the lowest I've been since I took over. I think my lads just thought they'd turn up and they'd win. But there was only one team in it and that was Gloucester.

Worse followed in the Conference, with another humiliating day for Woking fans when Morecambe slammed six second-half goals past their team at Kingfield without reply. The Cards had no game plan, played route one football and poor on-loan 'keeper Robert Burch from Spurs became the fourth Cards custodian to let in five or more during the season, Jalal having been ruled out with a thigh strain. Iraqi Jalal didn't play again all season, prompting rumours that the heightening crisis in his homeland, culminating in war, was the cause of his absence (which was wholly understandable).

Unadulterated joy as Martin Williams finds the net in the 2-2 draw with Doncaster Rovers.

With a daunting run-in from March onwards, Woking's chances of avoiding the drop seemed slim, given their recent form. Banger had departed, having become disil-lusioned with his lack of starts in the team, and Cockerill was happy to tear up the remaining two months of his contract to allow him to join Eastleigh. Cockerill was also happy to let Coates return to Swansea, the winger's influence not being as prominent as expected, while Scott Smith and Abbey both left, joining already departed Grant Payne, Rob Hollingdale and Dave Piper. Smith and Payne joined Scott Steele at Kingstonian.

But the likes of Ben Townsend, Dean Austin, Jamie Campbell and Martin Williams had been recruited and were all involved in the squad against champions elect Yeovil on 8 March. Everybody expected the worst, but a spirited 1-1 draw was just the tonic – Boardman's goal only the second from open play from a Woking defender all season.

Cockerill earmarked matches against Farnborough, Stevenage and Southport as the three wins which would keep the club up. But his team won none of them. However, an incredible run of nine straight draws, starting with that superb point against Yeovil and ending in the penultimate match at Barnet, beat the previous Conference record of seven and included excellent results against Doncaster, Halifax, Chester and Dagenham. The incredible drama at Chester summed up Woking's luck when they led 2-0 with three minutes remaining before letting in two goals and missing a penalty in the process. As if the season hadn't been eventful enough already.

Cockerill had by now brought in midfielder Scott Canham, on loan from Orient, the sort of creative influence the club had been craving all season. Fellow midfielder Dean Clark, a £3,500 purchase from Hayes, and Amos Foyewa, from Bournemouth, also

Warren Patmore and Raphael Nade threaten the Dagenham and Redbridge rearguard.

came in. Clint Davies, a goalkeeper on loan from Birmingham, replaced Burch (who had been recalled by Spurs) only to last two matches himself before Steve Bruce's outfit wanted him back at St Andrews. Ashley Bayes therefore became the sixth player to don the 'keeper's jersey during the season.

The talk of relegation had been rife for weeks, with Woking not being able to grab a win that had eluded them since 8 February. Now, on the very last day, it was win or bust – with a twist. Not only did Woking need to beat Telford at home, they must rely on other results. Either two from Leigh, Gravesend and Southport must not win, or Woking could afford for two of them to win if Nuneaton lost.

Inspired by Neil Smith, a superb performance saw Woking take a 3-0 lead midway through the second half, while rivals Stevenage were doing The Cards a favour by winning by the same score against Southport. Gravesend and Leigh were drawing 0-0 and Farnborough, with just thirteen fit players, were winning at Nuneaton, a match Cards' fans had almost discounted. Surely Nuneaton would get the point they needed on home soil. With many fans at Kingfield listening to commentator Nick Metcalfe on BBC Southern Counties radio, the tension became unbearable when it was announced that Leigh and Gravesend had both scored to lead 1-0. Now the Farnborough result was crucial. A couple of minutes later, Metcalfe's voice was tinged with alarm when he announced, "there's been a goal at Nuneaton". There were hushed tones around the ground as a goal for the home side at that point – with results staying the same elsewhere – would have sent Woking tumbling into the Ryman League. "And it's

It's all over; fans celebrate last-day survival after the 3-0 win against Telford United.

Nuneaton 0 Farnborough 2," cried Metcalfe – signalling a huge roar around the ground as the relief and joy kicked in.

The scorelines remained the same in all five matches from the moment former Cards' loan star Pitcher had thumped in Farnborough's second. That same player had saved Woking the previous season and here he was cementing their Conference place for 2003/04 – albeit indirectly. There had been talk of just one team being relegated and a league revamp with twenty-four teams for the following season but all the hype around that subject – and the worries about the club's abysmal goal difference, were rendered academic. The Cards had started the day one place off the bottom and had jumped two places to escape by a point. Kettering, Nuneaton and Southport – the latter having their first visit into the bottom three all season – were the doomed clubs. The irony of Woking's two biggest rivals, Stevenage and Farnborough, saving them from the drop was not lost on anybody connected with The Cards. And there had even been a roar at The Recreation Ground from supporters of promoted Ryman Leaguers Aldershot Town on hearing that arch-enemies Woking had survived, with hostilities between the two about to resume in league matches rather than one-off cup ties.

There were scenes of joy at Kingfield which could not be contained, while a sense of relief hung in the air – particularly with the end-of-season dinner arranged for that evening. "I never thought we'd go down," said Cockerill, while a relieved and jubilant Ingram could at least throw away one of his prepared speeches for the evening. Amid the euphoria it was pertinent to reflect that the club had achieved nothing. The long-ball tactics had alienated some fans and it seemed perverse to celebrate the mere act of survival.

Yes, the last day had been one hell of a party but things would have to change. Because one thing was for sure – nobody wanted to go through that again.

Statistics

1992/93

		Home					Away						
	P	W	D	L	F	A	W	D	L	F	A	GD	Pts
Wycombe Wanderers	42	13	5	3	46	16	11	6	4	38	21	47	83
Bromsgrove Rovers	42	9	7	5	35	22	9	7	5	32	27	18	68
Dagenham & Redbridge	42	10	5	6	48	29	9	6	6	27	18	28	67
Yeovil Town	42	13	5	3	42	21	5	7	9	17	28	10	66
Slough Town	42	12	3	6	39	28	6	8	7	21	27	5	65
Stafford Rangers	42	7	6	8	22	24	11	4	6	33	23	8	64
Bath City	42	9	8	4	29	23	6	6	9	24	23	7	59
Woking	**42**	**9**	**2**	**10**	**30**	**33**	**8**	**6**	**7**	**28**	**29**	**-4**	**59**
Kidderminster Harriers	42	9	5	7	26	30	5	11	5	34	30	0	58
Altrincham	42	7	7	7	21	25	8	6	7	28	27	3	58
Northwich Victoria	42	5	6	10	24	29	11	2	8	44	26	13	56
Stalybridge Celtic	42	7	10	4	25	26	6	7	8	23	29	7	56
Kettering Town	42	10	5	6	36	28	4	8	9	25	35	2	55
Gateshead	42	9	6	6	27	19	5	4	12	26	37	3	52
Telford United	42	9	5	7	31	24	5	5	11	24	36	5	52
Merthyr Tydfil	42	4	9	8	26	37	10	1	10	25	42	-28	52
Witton Albion	42	5	9	7	30	34	6	8	7	32	31	3	50
Macclesfield Town	42	7	9	5	23	20	5	4	12	17	30	-10	49
Runcorn	42	8	3	10	32	36	5	7	9	26	40	18	49
Welling United	42	8	6	7	34	37	4	6	11	23	35	15	48
Farnborough Town	42	8	5	8	34	36	4	6	11	34	51	-19	47
Boston United	42	5	6	10	23	31	4	7	10	27	38	19	40

Dagenham & Redbridge 1 point deducted.

1992/93

Players	Appearances	Goals Scored
Tim Alexander	29	
Trevor Baron	15	2
Laurence Batty	48	
Mark Biggins	34	6
Darren Broderick	3 (1)	
Dereck Brown	35 (4)	2
Kevan Brown	43	
Ansil Bushay	12	2
Richard Buzaglo	3 (1)	1
Tim Buzaglo	9(13)	5
Robbie Carroll	14 (8)	4
Andy Clement	26 (1)	3
David Coleman	6	1
Colin Fielder	33 (1)	1
Jon Finch	1	
Mark Fleming	33 (3)	5
David Greene	4 (2)	1
Danny Honey	1	
Brian Horne	1	
Tony Joyce	10	
Paul Kelly	1	
Steve Milton	4 (3)	2
Aidan Murphy	2	
Richard Nugent	40	3
Andy Pape	1	
Rob Peters	7	
Dave Puckett	34 (9)	12
Greg Roffe	2	
Zeke Rowe	1	
Trevor Senior	33 (7)	13
Scott Steele	27 (7)	5
Lloyd Wye	22	
Shane Wye	23	2

1993/94

	P	Home					Away					GD	Pts
		W	D	L	F	A	W	D	L	F	A		
Kidderminster Harriers	42	13	5	3	31	12	9	4	8	32	23	28	75
Kettering Town	42	9	7	5	23	14	10	8	3	23	10	22	72
Woking	**42**	**12**	**5**	**4**	**35**	**25**	**6**	**8**	**7**	**23**	**33**	**0**	**67**
Dagenham & Redbridge	42	12	5	4	41	23	3	9	9	21	31	8	59
Macclesfield Town	42	7	8	6	24	18	9	3	9	24	31	-1	59
Dover Athletic	42	9	3	9	28	24	8	4	9	20	25	-1	58
Stafford Rangers	42	10	7	4	39	22	4	8	9	17	30	4	57
Altrincham	42	8	5	8	23	22	8	4	9	18	20	-1	57
Gateshead	42	10	6	5	23	18	5	6	10	22	35	8	57
Bath City	42	6	8	7	28	21	7	9	5	19	17	9	56
Halifax Town	42	7	9	5	28	18	6	7	8	27	31	6	55
Stalybridge Celtic	42	6	6	9	27	30	8	6	7	27	25	-1	54
Northwich Victoria	42	7	9	5	26	19	4	10	7	18	26	-1	52
Welling United	42	7	7	7	25	23	6	5	10	22	26	-2	51
Telford United	42	8	7	6	24	22	5	5	11	17	27	8	51
Bromsgrove Rovers	42	5	8	8	26	32	7	5	7	28	34	-12	51
Yeovil Town	42	7	4	10	23	26	7	5	9	26	36	-13	51
Merthyr Tydfil	42	8	7	6	34	26	4	8	9	26	35	-1	49
Slough Town	42	8	8	5	30	24	3	6	12	14	34	-14	47
Witton Albion	42	4	8	9	18	30	3	5	13	19	33	-26	34

Merthyr Tydfil 2 points deducted.

1993/94

Players	Appearances	Goals Scored
Reuben Agboola	7	
Laurence Batty	55	
Gary Bennett	3	1
Gwynne Berry	56 (1)	
Mark Biggins	13 (8)	1
Delroy Brown	2 (4)	
Dereck Brown	57	4
Kevan Brown	58	4
Andy Clement	46	4
Jody Craddock	7	2
Lennie Dennis	25 (1)	13
Colin Fielder	34 (6)	
Dave Fleming	(3)	
Andy Gray	9 (1)	2
Dennis Greene	2 (1)	
Darran Hay	13	8
Paul Haylock	(1)	
Peter Heritage	3	
Connor Hislop	(5)	
Grant Hutchinson	(1)	
Barry Lakin	10 (5)	3
Ollie Morah	1	
Dave Puckett	21 (11)	5
Kevin Rattray	29 (9)	5
Tim Read	4	
Scott Steele	48 (4)	6
Kieran Swift	2 (4)	
Mark Tucker	40	2
Clive Walker	51 (1)	23
Lloyd Wye	36	2
Shane Wye	15	3

1994/95

		Home					Away						
	P	W	D	L	F	A	W	D	L	F	A	GD	Pts
Macclesfield Town	42	1	3	4	39	18	10	5	6	31	22	30	80
Woking	**42**	**11**	**8**	**2**	**46**	**23**	**10**	**4**	**7**	**30**	**31**	**22**	**75**
Southport	42	13	4	4	46	21	8	5	8	22	29	18	72
Altrincham	42	10	3	8	34	27	10	5	6	43	33	17	68
Stevenage Borough	42	10	4	7	40	27	10	3	8	28	22	19	67
Kettering Town	42	12	5	4	40	25	7	5	9	33	31	17	67
Gateshead	42	12	4	5	28	13	7	6	8	33	40	8	67
Halifax Town	42	11	6	4	46	20	6	6	9	22	34	14	63
Runcorn	42	11	7	3	39	28	5	3	13	20	43	12	58
Northwich Victoria	42	7	8	6	39	30	7	7	7	38	36	11	57
Kidderminster Harriers	42	6	5	10	28	29	10	4	7	35	32	2	57
Bath City	42	10	6	5	35	26	5	6	10	20	30	1	57
Bromsgrove Rovers	42	9	7	5	42	35	5	6	10	24	34	3	55
Farnborough Town	42	8	5	8	23	31	7	5	9	22	33	-19	55
Dagenham & Redbridge	42	8	5	8	28	32	5	8	8	28	37	-13	52
Dover Athletic	42	6	10	5	28	25	5	6	10	20	30	-7	49
Welling United	42	9	3	9	31	33	4	7	10	26	41	-17	49
Stalybridge Celtic	42	9	6	6	29	27	2	8	11	23	45	-20	47
Telford United	42	9	9	3	30	20	1	7	13	23	42	-9	46
Merthyr Tydfil	42	10	4	7	37	27	1	7	13	16	36	-10	44
Stafford Rangers	42	5	5	11	29	34	4	6	11	24	45	-26	38
Yeovil Town	42	5	8	8	29	31	3	6	12	21	40	-21	37

Yeovil Town 1 point deducted

1994/95

Players	Appearances	Goals Scored
Tim Alexander	9 (3)	
Laurence Batty	54	
Jim Benton	3	
Gwynne Berry	7 (2)	
Simon Brooks	1 (2)	
Dereck Brown	17 (3)	
Kevan Brown	53	
John Crumplin	15 (1)	1
Paul De Garis	1	
Lennie Dennis	14 (8)	9
Andy Ellis	38 (3)	4
Colin Fielder	57	5
Stuart Girdler	1 (4)	
David Greene	5 (1)	5
Darran Hay	29	19
Chris James	1 (3)	
Richard Newbery	3 (6)	1
Steve Parmenter	1	
Grant Payne	11 (1)	5
Kevin Rattray	29(14)	9
Craig Ravenscroft	2 (2)	
Tim Read	3 (3)	
Scott Steele	42 (2)	11
Lee Tierling	32 (5)	1
Dave Timothy	2 (2)	
Mark Tucker	57	4
Clive Walker	53	25
Lloyd Wye	49	1
Shane Wye	53	2

1995/96

	P	Home					Away					GD	Pts
		W	D	L	F	A	W	D	L	F	A		
Stevenage Borough	42	13	6	2	51	20	14	4	3	50	24	57	91
Woking	**42**	**16**	**5**	**0**	**47**	**13**	**9**	**3**	**9**	**36**	**41**	**29**	**83**
Hednesford Town	42	13	3	5	38	21	10	4	7	33	25	25	76
Macclesfield Town	42	12	5	4	32	16	10	4	7	34	33	17	75
Gateshead	42	9	7	5	32	24	9	6	6	26	22	12	67
Southport	42	10	7	4	42	25	8	5	8	35	39	13	66
Kidderminster Harriers	42	13	4	4	49	26	5	6	10	29	40	12	64
Northwich Victoria	42	9	3	9	38	35	7	9	5	34	29	8	60
Morecambe	42	12	2	7	51	33	5	6	10	27	39	6	59
Farnborough Town	42	8	6	7	29	23	7	8	6	34	35	5	59
Bromsgrove Rovers	42	11	6	4	33	20	4	8	9	26	37	2	59
Altrincham	42	9	6	6	33	29	6	7	8	26	35	-5	58
Telford United	42	8	7	6	27	23	7	3	11	24	33	-5	55
Stalybridge Celtic	42	9	3	9	29	37	7	4	10	30	31	-9	55
Halifax Town	42	8	7	6	30	25	5	6	10	19	38	-14	52
Kettering Town	42	9	5	7	38	32	4	4	13	30	52	-16	48
Slough Town	42	4	6	11	35	44	9	2	10	28	32	-13	47
Bath City	42	9	4	8	29	31	4	3	14	16	35	-21	46
Welling United	42	6	8	7	21	23	4	7	10	21	30	-11	45
Dover Athletic	42	8	1	12	29	38	3	6	12	22	36	-23	40
Runcorn	42	4	5	12	25	43	5	3	13	23	44	-39	35
Dagenham & Redbridge	42	5	7	9	31	34	2	5	14	12	39	-30	33

1995/96

Players	Appearances	Goals Scored
Darren Adams	4 (3)	3
Tim Alexander	1 (4)	
Trevor Baron	9 (2)	2
Laurence Batty	52	
Kevan Brown	50	2
Robert Codner	3 (1)	
John Crumplin	45	2
Julian Dowe	4 (1)	
Andy Ellis	53	9
Colin Fielder	54	3
Stuart Girdler	3 (13)	1
Neville Gordon	1 (1)	
John Gregory	3 (1)	
Darran Hay	40 (12)	22
Liburd Henry	1 (1)	
Carl Hoddle	4	
Junior Hunter	12 (2)	14
Aiden Kilner	(2)	
Gary Lansdown	(1)	
Joe Omigie	1 (3)	
Rob Peters	2 (5)	1
Craig Rainbow	1 (1)	1
Nicky Reid	12 (3)	1
Scott Steele	38 (1)	18
Steve Thompson	36 (1)	2
Lee Tierling	4 (3)	
Dave Timothy	24 (7)	
Mark Tucker	43	1
Clive Walker	44 (1)	23
Paul Wanless	5	1
Lloyd Wye	37 (1)	3

1996/97

		Home						Away				GD	Pts
	P	W	D	L	F	A	W	D	L	F	A		
Macclesfield.Town	42	15	4	2	41	11	12	5	4	39	19	50	90
Kidderminster Harriers	42	14	4	3	48	18	12	3	6	36	24	42	85
Stevenage Borough	42	15	4	2	53	23	9	6	6	34	30	34	82
Morecambe	42	10	5	6	34	23	9	4	8	35	33	13	66
Woking	**42**	**10**	**5**	**6**	**41**	**29**	**8**	**5**	**8**	**30**	**34**	**8**	**64**
Northwich Victoria	42	11	5	5	31	20	6	7	8	30	34	7	63
Farnborough Town	42	9	6	6	35	29	7	7	7	23	24	5	61
Hednesford Town	42	10	7	4	28	17	6	5	10	24	33	2	60
Telford United	42	6	7	8	21	30	10	3	8	25	26	-10	58
Gateshead	42	8	6	7	32	27	7	5	9	27	36	-4	56
Southport	42	8	5	8	27	28	7	5	9	24	33	-10	55
Rushden & Diamonds	42	8	8	5	30	25	6	3	12	31	38	-2	53
Stalybridge Celtic	42	9	5	7	35	29	5	5	11	18	29	-5	52
Kettering Town	42	9	4	8	30	28	5	5	11	23	34	-9	51
Hayes	42	7	7	7	27	21	5	7	9	27	34	-1	50
Slough Town	42	7	7	7	42	32	5	7	9	20	33	-3	50
Dover Athletic	42	7	9	5	32	30	5	5	11	25	38	-11	50
Welling United	42	9	2	10	24	26	4	7	10	26	34	-10	48
Halifax Town	42	9	5	7	39	37	3	7	11	16	37	-19	48
Bath City	42	9	5	7	27	28	3	6	12	26	52	-27	47
Bromsgrove Rovers	42	8	4	9	29	30	4	1	16	12	37	-26	41
Altrincham	42	6	3	12	25	34	3	9	9	24	39	-24	39

1996/97

Players	Appearances	Goals Scored
Laurence Batty	46	1
Kevin Betsy	1 (1)	
Simon Brooks	1	
Kevan Brown	57	
Andy Ellis	35 (7)	5
Lee Ellison	1 (1)	
Colin Fielder	9 (1)	
Steve Foster	40	3
Simon Garner	(5)	
Giuliano Grazioli	6	6
John Gregory	11 (2)	
Darran Hay	25 (16)	13
Terry Howard	44 (1)	1
Junior Hunter 16 (14)	3	
Paul Hyde	1 app	
Justin Jackson	20 (2)	4
Tom Jones	40 (6)	2
Ben Kamara	2 (3)	
Tony Kelly	1	
Aiden Kilner	2(3)	1
Lee Palmer	7	
Grant Payne	4	1
Steve Sailsman	1	
Hans Segers	1	
Scott Steele	44 (5)	16
Robin Taylor	41 (10)	6
Steve Thompson	51	7
Dave Timothy	13 (6)	1
Clive Walker	52 (1)	20
Steve Wood	7	
Lloyd Wye	25 (9)	
Shane Wye	42	2

1997/98

	P	Home						Away					GD	Pts
		W	D	L	F	A		W	D	L	F	A		
Halifax Town	42	17	4	0	51	15		8	8	5	23	28	31	87
Cheltenham Town	42	15	4	2	39	15		8	5	8	24	28	20	78
Woking	**42**	**14**	**3**	**4**	**47**	**22**		**8**	**5**	**8**	**25**	**24**	**26**	**74**
Rushden & Diamonds	42	12	4	5	44	26		11	1	9	35	31	22	74
Morecambe	42	11	4	6	35	30		10	6	5	42	34	13	73
Hereford United	42	11	7	3	30	19		7	6	8	26	30	7	67
Hednesford Town	42	14	4	3	28	12		4	8	9	31	38	9	66
Slough Town	42	10	6	5	34	21		8	4	9	24	28	9	64
Northwich Victoria	42	8	9	4	34	24		7	6	8	29	35	4	60
Welling United	43	11	5	6	42	32		6	4	11	25	35	0	60
Yeovil Town	42	14	3	4	45	24		3	5	13	28	39	10	59
Hayes	42	10	4	7	36	25		6	6	9	26	27	10	58
Dover Athletic	42	10	4	7	34	29		5	6	10	26	41	-10	55
Southport	42	9	5	7	32	26		5	6	11	29	35	0	53
Kettering Town	42	8	6	7	29	29		5	7	9	24	31	-7	52
Stevenage Borough	42	8	8	5	35	27		5	4	12	24	36	-4	51
Kidderminster Harriers	42	6	8	7	32	31		5	6	10	24	3	-7	47
Farnborough Town	42	10	3	8	37	27		2	5	14	19	43	-14	44
Leek Town	42	8	8	5	34	26		2	6	13	18	41	-15	44
Telford United	42	6	7	8	25	31		4	5	12	28	45	-23	42
Gateshead	42	7	6	8	32	35		1	5	15	19	52	-36	35
Stalybridge Celtic	42	6	5	10	33	38		1	3	17	15	55	-45	29

1997/98

Players	Appearances	Goals Scored
Nathan Abbey	5	
Dante Alighieri	(1)	
Laurence Batty	51	
Kevin Betsy	50 (3)	6
Kevan Brown	34 (1)	
Michael Danzey	34 (2)	3
Andy Ellis	42 (4)	
Jon French	1	
Stuart Girdler	2 (3)	
Richard Goddard	9	
Darran Hay	39 (6)	23
Andy Hayward	8	5
Terry Howard	16 (1)	1
Junior Hunter	1	
Justin Jackson	9	1
Tom Jones	11 (3)	
Ben Kamara	11 (4)	
Aiden Kilner	1 (6)	
Rod McAree	13 (4)	4
Grant Payne	46 (5)	19
Eddie Saunders	35	2
Stuart Searle	4	
Scott Smith	36 (10)	2
Scott Steele	42 (9)	9
Simon Stewart	7	
Wayne Sutton	27 (2)	2
Robin Taylor	40 (1)	3
Steve Thompson	33	3
David Timothy	33	3
Steve West	26 (9)	17
Steve Wood	1	

1998/99

	P	Home						Away						GD	Pts
		W	D	L	F	A	W	D	L	F	A				
Cheltenham Town	42	11	9	1	35	14	11	5	5	36	22			35	80
Kettering Town	42	11	5	5	31	16	11	5	5	27	21			21	76
Hayes	42	12	3	6	34	25	10	5	6	29	25			13	74
Rushden & Diamonds	42	11	4	6	41	22	9	8	4	30	20			29	72
Yeovil Town	42	8	4	9	35	32	12	7	2	33	22			14	71
Stevenage Borough	42	9	9	3	37	23	8	8	5	25	22			17	68
Northwich Victoria	42	11	3	7	29	21	8	6	7	31	30			9	66
Kingstonian	42	9	7	5	25	19	8	6	7	25	30			1	64
Woking	**42**	**9**	**5**	**7**	**27**	**20**	**9**	**4**	**8**	**24**	**25**			**6**	**63**
Hednesford Town	42	9	8	4	30	24	6	8	7	19	20			5	61
Dover Athletic	42	7	9	5	27	21	8	4	9	27	27			6	58
Forest Green Rovers	42	9	5	7	28	22	6	8	7	27	28			5	58
Hereford United	42	9	5	7	25	17	6	5	10	24	29			3	55
Morecambe	42	9	5	7	31	29	6	3	12	29	47			-16	53
Kidderminster Harriers	42	9	4	8	32	22	5	5	11	24	30			4	51
Doncaster Rovers	42	7	5	9	26	26	5	7	9	25	29			-4	48
Telford United	42	7	8	6	24	24	3	8	10	20	36			-16	46
Southport	42	6	9	6	29	28	4	6	11	18	31			-12	45
Barrow	42	7	5	9	17	23	4	5	12	23	40			-23	43
Welling United	42	4	7	10	18	30	5	7	9	26	35			-21	41
Leek Town	42	5	5	11	34	42	3	3	15	14	34			-28	32
Farnborough Town	42	6	5	10	29	48	1	6	14	12	41			-48	32

1998/99

Players	Appearances	Goals Scored
Dante Alighieri	3	
Laurence Batty	39	
Kevin Betsy	7	2
Danny Bolt	37 (11)	9
Ronell Coward	1 (6)	2
Michael Danzey	45	2
Andy Ellis	36 (10)	3
Darryl Flahavan	19	
Steve French	8 (4)	
Stuart Girdler	38 (4)	1
Richard Goddard	15	2
Phil Gridelet	22	1
Darran Hay	37 (11)	25
Rob Hollingdale	41	1
Ben Kamara	3 (3)	
Rod McAree	(1)	
Damian Panter	(1)	
Grant Payne	42 (8)	16
Steve Perkins	29 (3)	4
Eddie Saunders	47 (1)	1
Scott Smith	53	
Brian Statham	6	
Scott Steele	36 (8)	4
Wayne Sutton	6	
Robin Taylor	22 (1)	1
David Timothy	1 (3)	
Steve West	38 (9)	13

1999/20

	P	Home					Away					GD	Pts
		W	D	L	F	A	W	D	L	F	A		
Kidderminster Harriers	42	16	3	2	47	16	10	4	7	28	24	35	85
Rushden & Diamonds	42	11	8	2	37	18	10	5	6	34	24	29	76
Morecambe	42	10	7	4	46	29	8	9	4	24	19	22	70
Scarborough	42	10	6	5	36	14	9	6	6	24	21	25	69
Kingstonian	42	9	4	8	30	24	11	3	7	28	20	14	67
Dover Athletic	42	10	7	4	43	26	8	5	8	22	30	9	66
Yeovil Town	42	11	4	6	37	28	7	6	8	23	35	-3	64
Hereford United	42	9	6	6	43	31	6	8	7	18	21	9	59
Southport	42	10	5	6	31	21	5	8	8	24	35	-1	58
Stevenage Borough	42	8	5	8	26	20	8	4	9	34	34	6	57
Hayes	42	7	3	11	24	28	9	5	7	33	30	-1	56
Doncaster Rovers	42	7	5	9	19	21	8	4	9	27	27	-2	54
Kettering Town	42	8	5	3	25	19	4	6	11	19	31	-6	52
Woking	**42**	**5**	**6**	**10**	**17**	**27**	**8**	**7**	**6**	**28**	**26**	**-8**	**52**
Nuneaton Borough	42	7	6	8	28	25	5	9	7	21	28	-4	51
Telford United	42	12	4	5	34	21	2	5	14	22	45	-10	51
Hednesford Town	42	10	3	8	27	23	5	3	13	18	45	-23	51
Northwich Victoria	42	10	8	3	33	25	3	4	14	20	53	-25	51
Forest Green Rovers	42	11	2	8	35	23	2	6	13	19	40	-9	47
Welling United	42	6	5	10	27	32	7	3	11	27	34	-12	47
Altrincham	42	6	8	7	31	26	3	11	7	20	34	-9	46
Sutton United	42	4	8	9	23	32	4	2	15	16	43	-36	34

1999/20

Players	Appearances	Goals Scored
Nassim Akrour	46 (5)	19
Dante Alighieri	11 (4)	
Laurence Batty	19	
Danny Bolt	10 (19)	4
Kevan Brown	13 (1)	
Michael Bullen	(1)	
Julian Charles	4 (8)	
Michael Danzey	30	1
Darryl Flahavan	36 (2)	
Steve French	1	
Stuart Girdler	17 (6)	
Richard Goddard	14 (7)	2
Phil Gridelet	17 (1)	
Matt Hayfield	14 (1)	3
Darran Hay	30 (9)	16
Iain Hendry	1	
Rob Hollingdale	43 (1)	
Barry Miller	17	
Damian Panter	5 (6)	1
Grant Payne	10 (4)	4
Steve Perkins	41 (3)	4
Eddie Saunders	6 (1)	
Robert Simpson	2	1
Peter Smith	25 (2)	
Rob Smith	9 (1)	
Scott Smith	49	
Scott Steele	36 (5)	6
Steve Stott	9 (1)	
Steve West	47 (1)	9
Reece White	(1)	
Darron Wilkinson	32 (11)	

2000/01

	P	Home					Away					GD	Pts
		W	D	L	F	A	W	D	L	F	A		
Rushden & Diamonds	42	14	6	1	41	13	11	5	5	37	23	42	86
Yeovil Town	42	14	3	4	41	17	10	5	6	32	33	23	80
Dagenham & Redbridge	42	13	4	4	39	19	10	4	7	32	35	17	77
Southport	42	9	5	7	33	24	11	4	6	25	22	12	69
Leigh RMI	42	11	5	5	38	24	8	6	7	25	33	6	68
Telford United	42	13	1	7	33	23	6	7	8	18	28	0	65
Stevenage Borough	42	8	7	6	36	33	7	11	3	35	28	10	63
Chester City	42	9	8	4	29	19	7	6	8	20	24	6	62
Doncaster Rovers	42	11	5	5	28	17	4	8	9	19	26	4	58
Scarborough	42	7	9	5	29	25	7	7	7	27	29	2	58
Hereford United	42	6	12	3	27	19	8	3	10	33	27	14	57
Boston United	42	10	7	4	43	28	3	10	8	31	35	11	56
Nuneaton Borough	42	9	5	7	35	26	4	10	7	25	34	0	54
Woking	**42**	**5**	**10**	**6**	**30**	**30**	**8**	**5**	**8**	**22**	**27**	**-5**	**54**
Dover Athletic	42	9	6	6	32	22	5	5	11	22	34	-2	53
Forest Green Rovers	42	6	9	6	28	28	5	6	10	15	26	-11	48
Northwich Victoria	42	8	7	6	31	24	3	6	12	18	43	-18	46
Hayes	42	5	6	10	22	31	7	4	10	22	40	-27	46
Morecambe	42	8	5	8	35	29	3	7	11	29	37	-2	45
Kettering Town	42	5	5	11	23	31	6	5	10	23	31	-16	43
Kingstonian	42	3	5	13	19	40	5	5	11	28	33	-26	34
Hednesford Town	42	2	6	13	24	38	3	7	11	22	48	-40	28

2000/01

Players	Appearances	Goals Scored
Dante Alighieri	3 (6)	
Luke Basford	3	
Stuart Baverstock	4	
Jon Boardman	9	
Kevan Brown	13 (4)	
Daniel Costello	2	
Paulo Da Costa	1 (3)	2
Matthew Davies	1	
Gary Drewett	(1)	
Mark Druce	5 (5)	2
Luke Edghill	1 (1)	
Darryl Flahavan	7	
Matthew Fowler	(2)	
Steve French	1 (1)	
Adie Graham	(1)	
Charlie Griffin	28 (3)	14
Matt Hayfield	32 (4)	2
Rob Hollingdale	40 (2)	
Junior Kadi	11 (11)	2
Caleb Kamara-Taylor	1 (3)	
Jae Martin	5	
Vince Matassa	29	
Mark McGhee	(1)	
Christian Metcalfe	4 (2)	
Lee O'Donnell	3 (1)	2
Mark Ormerod	10	
Damian Panter	(3)	
Steve Perkins	39 (7)	3
Jamie Pitman	31 (2)	3
Stuart Reeks	8 (3)	
Nick Roddis	39 (2)	
Phil Ruggles	3 (3)	1
Chris Sharpling	14	9
Scott Smith	37 (1)	
Paul Steele	6	1
Scott Steele	42 (4)	11
Richard Taylor	5	
Simon Teague	5 (16)	
Mark Watson	9 (6)	1
Mike Webb	1	
Steve West	44 (2)	4
Darron Wilkinson	2 (1)	
Chris Woodcock	2	
Ben Wright	3 (1)	
Shane Wye	20	

2001/02

	P	Home					Away					GD	Pts
		W	D	L	F	A	W	D	L	F	A		
Boston United	42	12	5	4	53	24	13	4	4	31	18	42	84
Dagenham & Redbridge	42	13	6	2	35	20	11	6	4	35	27	23	84
Yeovil Town	42	6	7	8	27	30	13	6	2	39	23	13	70
Doncaster Rovers	42	11	6	4	41	23	7	7	7	27	23	22	67
Barnet	42	10	4	7	30	19	9	6	6	34	29	16	67
Morecambe	42	12	5	4	30	27	5	6	10	33	40	-4	62
Farnborough Town	42	11	3	7	38	23	7	4	10	28	31	12	61
Margate	42	7	9	5	33	22	7	7	7	26	31	6	58
Telford United	42	8	6	7	34	31	6	9	6	29	27	5	57
Nuneaton Borough	42	9	3	9	33	27	7	6	8	24	30	0	57
Stevenage Borough	42	10	4	7	36	30	5	6	10	21	30	-3	55
Scarborough	42	9	6	6	27	22	5	8	8	28	41	-8	55
Northwich Victoria	42	9	4	8	32	34	7	3	11	25	36	-13	55
Chester City	42	7	7	7	40	26	4	8	9	13	23	4	53
Leigh RMI	42	6	4	11	29	29	9	4	8	27	29	-2	53
Hereford United	42	9	6	6	28	15	5	4	12	22	38	-3	52
Forest Green Rovers	42	7	7	7	28	32	5	8	8	26	44	-22	51
Woking	**42**	**7**	**5**	**9**	**28**	**29**	**6**	**4**	**11**	**31**	**41**	**-11**	**48**
Hayes	42	6	2	13	27	45	7	3	11	26	35	-27	44
Stalybridge Celtic	42	7	6	8	26	32	4	4	13	14	37	-29	43
Dover Athletic	42	6	5	10	20	25	5	1	15	21	4	-24	39

2001/02

Players	Appearances	Goals Scored
Jon Allman	(2)	
Stuart Baverstock	2	
Scott Bevan	7	
Jon Boardman	13 (1)	1
Dean Chandler	16	1
Julian Capone	2	
Roscoe D'Sane	16 (6)	5
Murray Fishlock	1	
Michael Fowler	9 (2)	
Gareth Graham	3 (3)	
Charlie Griffin	25 (11)	12
Warren Haughton	9 (13)	6
Rob Hollingdale	18	
Scott Huckerby	6 (6)	3
Junior Kadi	7 (6)	1
Terry McFlynn	5 (5)	1
Brian McGorry	2	
Barry Moore	42 (1)	8
Warren Patmore	25 (6)	13
Steve Perkins	30 (8)	3
David Piper	50	
Geoff Pitcher	15	2
Jamie Pitman	25 (2)	
Martin Randall	(3)	
Dominic Reece	16 (1)	
Stuart Reeks	17 (6)	
Nick Roddis	10 (1)	1
Phil Ruggles	1 (1)	1
Eddie Saunders	19 (3)	1
Chris Sharpling	33 (3)	10
Scott Smith	36 (2)	2
Paul Steele	9 (1)	
Scott Steele	21 (7)	3
Tony Tucker	42	
Lloyd Webber	4 (2)	
Steve West	24 (2)	5

2002/03

	P	Home					Away					GD	Pts
		W	D	L	F	A	W	D	L	F	A		
Yeovil Town	42	16	5	0	54	13	12	6	3	46	24	63	95
Morecambe	42	17	3	1	52	13	6	6	9	34	29	44	78
Doncaster Rovers	42	11	6	4	28	17	11	6	4	45	30	26	78
Chester City	42	10	6	5	36	21	11	6	4	23	10	28	75
Dagenham & Redbridge	42	12	5	4	38	23	9	4	8	33	36	12	72
Hereford United	42	9	5	7	36	22	10	2	9	28	29	13	64
Scarborough	42	12	3	6	41	28	6	7	8	22	26	9	64
Halifax Town	42	11	5	5	34	28	7	5	9	16	23	-1	64
Forest Green Rovers	42	12	3	6	41	29	5	5	11	20	33	-1	59
Margate	42	8	9	4	32	24	7	2	12	28	42	-6	56
Barnet	42	9	4	8	32	28	4	10	7	33	40	-3	53
Stevenage Borough	42	7	6	8	31	25	7	4	10	30	30	6	52
Farnborough Town	42	8	6	7	37	29	5	6	10	20	27	1	51
Northwich Victoria	42	6	5	10	26	34	7	7	7	40	38	-6	51
Telford United	42	7	2	12	20	33	7	5	9	34	36	-15	49
Burton Albion	42	6	6	9	25	31	7	4	10	27	46	-25	49
Gravesend & Northfleet	42	8	5	8	37	35	4	7	10	25	38	-11	48
Leigh RMI	42	8	5	8	26	34	6	1	14	18	37	-27	48
Woking	**42**	**8**	**7**	**6**	**30**	**35**	**3**	**7**	**11**	**22**	**46**	**-29**	**47**
Nuneaton Borough	42	9	4	8	27	32	4	3	14	24	46	-27	46
Southport	42	6	8	7	31	32	5	4	12	23	37	-15	45
Kettering Town	42	4	3	14	23	39	4	4	13	14	34	-36	31

2002/03

Players	Appearances	Goals Scored
Ben Abbey	23 (3)	9
Anthony Allman	17 (5)	
Dean Austin	18	2
Nicky Banger	15 (10)	4
Ashley Bayes	5	
Jon Boardman	45 (1)	1
Jon Brady	12	1
Robert Burch	6	
Wayne Burnett	3	
Jamie Campbell	13	
Scott Canham	10	2
Dean Clark	2 (4)	
Jonathan Coates	18 (2)	1
Glenn Cockerill	1	
Chris Collins	22 (1)	1
Jamal Da Costa	1 (2)	
Clint Davies	2	
Sean Evers	5 (1)	
Steve Farrelly	11 (1)	
Amos Foyewa	3 (4)	3
Ian Hamilton	24 (1)	
Shwan Jalal	23	
Robert Kember	30 (2)	1
Barry Moore	14 (1)	2
Raphael Nade	24	3
Warren Patmore	33 (8)	16
Grant Payne	3 (15)	2
David Piper	14 (7)	
Stuart Reeks	10 (6)	
Simon Rodger	1	
Lee Sandford	12	
Chris Sharpling	28 (9)	5
Ian Simpemba	17	1
Neil Smith	25 (1)	
Scott Smith	16 (8)	
Paul Steele	4 (1)	
Scott Steele	3 (2)	
Ben Townsend	18	1
Tony Tucker	2	
Tom White	2	
Martin Williams	5 (6)	1

Clive Walker and Scott Steele celebrate Woking's magnificent win against Cambridge in the second round of the FA Cup, December 1996.